Table of Contents

ⓘ Introduction v

① Parenting on Purpose: 1
Define Your Mission

② Growing Up 19
Connected

③ Safety Must Be 43
Prioritized

④ Be Aware: Anxiety, ... 63
Addiction & Reputation

⑤ Social 81
Media

⑥ Digital 89
Leadership

⑦ When the Ambulance 113
is Necessary

Connected: Parenting Faithfully in the Digital Age

Copyright © 2024 by Kaio Publications
http://www.kaiopublications.org

All rights reserved. No part of this publication may be reproduced, stored in a retrieval system, or transmitted in any form by any means, electronic, mechanical, photocopy, recording, or otherwise, without the prior permission of the author, except as provided for by USA copyright law.

First printing 2024
Printed in the United States of America

Scripture quotations taken from the New American Standard Bible® (NASB), Copyright © 1960, 1962, 1963, 1968, 1971, 1972, 1973, 1975, 1977, 1995 by The Lockman Foundation
Used by permission. www.Lockman.org.

ISBN: 978-1-952955-51-8

Grammar edited by Tonja McRady
Cover and interior design by Kristin Arbuckle

Introduction

If you've lived any amount of time, you know that technology has significantly changed over the years. I remember when I was in seventh grade in 1991 and learned how to type on an old Apple green screen computer. We learned programing by making our names float across the screen. At that time, our computer paper was connected with perforations, and it had the sides that the machine would grab to feed the paper through the printer. We made a lot of banners with the letter X because at that time, your images were all just Xs that were positioned to form a picture or spell a name.

I remember in 1995 when the internet was made available to the mass public. When the dial-up was attempting to connect the computer to the internet, the sound roared and shrilled as if the telephone line was going to burst through the wall. However, to describe this to children of a younger generation is almost an impossible task as they struggle to grasp what a world without internet would have been like. They don't know what you're talking about, and honestly, why should they? It is not their reality.

The truth is, for many parents of young children today, it's not your reality either. You've heard your parents describe what it was like; however, with the speed of technological advancements, having to wait on dial-up internet connections is in the same category as Civil War history or the Cold War. So if you're in that age group and you're thinking, "I don't understand anything of what you're saying," that's okay. The moment that we think we have learned enough to write a book on the subject, technology has already quickly changed and new possibilities, obstacles, and concerns have been born.

In the world of parenting, the digital age presents a landscape that is both exciting and daunting. As parents, we are witnessing unprecedented changes in how our children interact with the world, learn, communicate, and form relationships. The digital revolution has brought with it a host of opportunities—educational resources at our fingertips, instant communication with loved ones, and a global community that transcends borders. But alongside these opportunities come significant challenges: the pervasive influence of social media, the constant presence of screens, the risks of online predators, and the potential for addiction to digital devices.

For Christian parents, these challenges are not just about managing technology; they are about nurturing our children's souls in a world that often seems to pull them away from God's truth. How do we guide our children to live faithfully in a world where they are constantly bombarded with messages that contradict Biblical values? How do we teach them to discern truth from falsehood, to value real relationships over virtual ones, and to find their identity in Christ rather than in the number of likes they receive on social media?

This book is a journey into faithful parenting in the digital age, a journey that starts with understanding the world our children are growing up in and ends with equipping them to navigate it with wisdom and grace. As we embark on this journey together, let us remember that our ultimate goal is not just to raise children who are tech-savvy, but to raise children who are God-centered. We want to instill in them the ability to use technology as a tool for good rather than allowing it to become a stumbling block in their spiritual walk.

The Digital Landscape: A World of Change

The digital age is characterized by rapid technological advancements that have transformed nearly every aspect of our lives. Smartphones, tablets, laptops, and other devices are now integral parts of daily life, and—for many families—they are present from morning until night. Our children are growing up as digital natives—never knowing a world without the internet, social media, or instant access to information.

With this digital immersion comes a shift in how children perceive the world around them. They are constantly connected yet often feel more isolated than ever before. They have access to vast amounts of information yet struggle with misinformation and the pressure to conform to online standards. The digital age has given them unprecedented opportunities for learning and creativity, but it has also introduced new avenues for distraction and temptation.

As Christian parents, we are called to navigate this landscape with discernment. We must be aware of the ways in which technology can shape our children's worldview, influence their values, and impact their spiritual growth. This requires more than just setting limits on screen time; it requires a proactive approach to teaching our children how to engage with technology in a way that honors God.

The Call to Faithful Parenting

In Deuteronomy 6:6-7, we are given a clear mandate as parents: *"These commandments that I give you today are to be on your hearts. Impress them on your children. Talk about them when you sit at home and when you walk along the road, when you lie down and when you get up."* This passage reminds us that our primary responsibility as parents is to teach our children about God and His commandments. This task does not change with the advent of new technology; rather, it becomes even more critical.

Faithful parenting in the digital age means that we must be intentional in how we teach our children to live out their faith in a world that is increasingly hostile to Christian values. It means helping them to understand that their worth is not determined by their online presence but by their identity as children of God. It means guiding them to make choices that reflect their commitment to Christ, even when those choices are difficult or countercultural.

This book is grounded in the belief that God's Word is timeless and that its principles are applicable in every age, including our own. As we explore the challenges and opportunities of parenting in the digital age, we will do so through the lens of Scripture, seeking God's wisdom and guidance at every turn. Our goal is to equip you, as parents, with the tools and knowledge you need to raise your children in a way that is both faithful to God and responsive to the realities of the digital world.

The Role of Technology in Our Lives

One of the first steps in navigating the digital age as Christian parents is to recognize the role that technology plays in our own lives. It's easy to point fingers at our children's use of technology, but we must first examine how we are using it ourselves. Are we modeling healthy, God-honoring behavior when it comes to our own screen time? Do we allow technology to interfere with our relationships, our work, or our spiritual lives?

In Matthew 7:3-5, Jesus warns against the hypocrisy of pointing out the speck in someone else's eye while ignoring the plank in our own. In the context of parenting, this means that we must be willing to address our own habits and attitudes toward technology before we can effectively guide our children. By modeling responsible and intentional use of technology, we set an example for our children to follow.

This also means that we must be willing to set boundaries for ourselves and our families. Just as we establish rules and guidelines for our children's use of technology, we must also establish them for ourselves. This might mean setting aside specific times for family devotions, meals, and other activities where technology is put aside in favor of face-to-face interaction. It might mean being intentional about how we use social media, ensuring that our online behavior reflects our commitment to Christ.

Teaching Discernment and Wisdom

One of the greatest challenges of the digital age is the sheer volume of information that is available to our children. With just a few clicks, they can access an endless stream of content—some of it good, some of it harmful, and much of it somewhere in between. As parents, we cannot shield our children from every negative influence, but we can equip them with the tools they need to discern truth from falsehood and to make wise decisions.

Proverbs 2:6 tells us, *"For the Lord gives wisdom; from his mouth come knowledge and understanding."* Teaching our children to seek wisdom from God's Word is one of the most important things we can do as parents. This involves more than just telling them what to think; it involves teaching them how to think critically and biblically. We want our children to be able to evaluate the messages they encounter in the digital world, to recognize when something is not aligned with God's truth, and to respond in a way that reflects their faith.

This discernment also extends to their interactions with others online. In a world where bullying, gossip, and negativity are rampant, we must teach our children to use their words to build others up, not tear them down. We must encourage them to be kind, compassionate, and respectful in all their online interactions, remembering that they are ambassadors for Christ in every aspect of their lives, including their digital presence.

Building Real Relationships in a Virtual World

One of the paradoxes of the digital age is that while it has made it easier than ever to connect with others, it has also led to a decline in meaningful, face-to-face relationships. Social media allows us to stay in touch with friends and family, but it can also create a false sense of connection that leaves us feeling empty and isolated. For children and teenagers who are still developing their social and emotional skills, this can be particularly damaging.

As Christian parents, we must prioritize real, meaningful relationships for our children. This means encouraging them to spend time with friends and family in person, to engage in activities that promote teamwork and cooperation, and to cultivate relationships that are grounded in mutual respect and love. It also means being present in our children's lives, taking the time to listen to them, talk with them, and pray with them.

Hebrews 10:24-25 reminds us, *"And let us consider how we may spur one another on toward love and good deeds, not giving up meeting together, as some are in the habit of doing, but encouraging one another."* In the digital age, this means not only gathering together as a church community but also fostering an environment in our homes where relationships are nurtured and where the love of Christ is evident in our interactions with one another.

The Power of Prayer

As we navigate the challenges of parenting in the digital age, we must never forget the power of prayer. Raising children in today's world can feel overwhelming at times, but we are not in this alone. God is with us, and He has given us the gift of prayer as a means of seeking His guidance, wisdom, and strength.

Philippians 4:6-7 encourages us, *"Do not be anxious about anything, but in every situation, by prayer and petition, with thanksgiving, present your requests to God. And the peace of God, which transcends all understanding, will guard your hearts and your minds in Christ Jesus."* As parents, we must bring our concerns, our fears, and our hopes for our children to God in prayer, trusting that He will provide us with the wisdom and grace we need.

This book will provide practical advice and strategies for parenting in the digital age, but we must remember that our ultimate source of strength and guidance comes from God. As we seek to raise our children to be faithful followers of Christ in a digital world, let us do so with hearts that are devoted to prayer, trusting that God is faithful and that He will guide us every step of the way.

A Journey of Faith

Parenting in the digital age is a journey, and like any journey, it will have its challenges and its rewards. There will be times when we feel unsure of how to proceed, when we make mistakes, and when we question whether we are doing enough. But through it all, we can have confidence that God is with us, guiding us and giving us the strength we need to fulfill the calling He has placed on our lives.

As we embark on this journey together, let us remember that our goal is not just to raise children who are successful in the eyes of the world, but to raise children who love God with all their hearts, who seek to live according to His Word, and who are equipped to navigate the digital world with wisdom and discernment. This is a high calling, but it is also a rewarding one, for as we invest in the spiritual growth of our children, we are investing in something that will last for eternity.

In the pages that follow, we will explore the various aspects of parenting in the digital age—from setting boundaries and teaching discernment to fostering real relationships and modeling godly behavior. Along the way, we will draw on the wisdom of Scripture and the experiences of Christian parents who have walked this path before us. Our prayer is that this book will be a source of encouragement, guidance, and hope as you seek to raise your children in a way that is faithful to God and responsive to the challenges of the digital age.

Let us begin this journey together, with hearts that are open to God's leading and with a commitment to raising our children in the nurture and admonition of the Lord. May God bless you as you seek to parent faithfully in the digital age.

1
Parenting on Purpose: Define Your Mission

As we begin this chapter, I want to introduce you to a few words and ask you to engage in a mental word association exercise. You don't have to answer out loud, although that would be funny to those around you observing you read this. Instead, I want you to think about what you read and what comes to your mind when you see these words.

Intentional

What's the first thing that comes to your mind when you read this word? While you think about that, I want you to think about another word, an antonym to intentional if you will. The word is accidental. *Merriam-Webster's Online Dictionary* defines it as "occurring unexpectedly or by chance; happening without intent or through carelessness and often with unfortunate results."[1] It's the concept that encompasses a "happy-go-lucky" lifestyle where sometimes the results of a decision or circumstance turn out ok and at other times, they don't turn out very well. Considering the definition of *accidental* while pondering the word *intentional* might bring clarity. Intentionality is the exact opposite of accidental. It is not careless. It's well thought through and has aim. Some would suggest that something that is intentional is also deliberate.

Deliberate

What comes to your mind when you hear the word *deliberate*? It also encompasses thoughtful consideration before acting. You don't simply react; you are proactive. You devote time to thinking thoroughly about your decision and actions before engaging. You consider what the ramifications might be if you took course number one, and you think about the outcomes if you take course number two. We understand this word, especially when it comes to money and money management. If I buy something, then that purchase impacts how much money we have remaining and what else, if anything, we would be able to purchase.

Purposed

What comes to your mind when you read the word *purposed*? The word literally means "something set up as an object or end to be attained."[2] In other words, we didn't accidentally end up where we are. Rather, we purposed to end up where we are. We didn't accidentally turn that TV show on. The TV is on because someone pushed the button on the remote control or told Alexa what to do.

Some of you have traveled quite extensively, and you know that before you can board an airplane you have to buy a ticket. You select when you want to fly out and to what destination you are going. With so many planes taking off and landing daily, we can only imagine the confusion that would exist if flight control towers weren't functioning in a very organized manner. It's such tremendous organization that with little to no problems, the control towers can manage the hundreds of planes which are landing and taking off every day. In most cases, with an element of professional certainty, they hit their mark on time.

I also travel a lot, and I've never boarded a plane for Dallas, Texas, and ended up in San Diego, California. Maybe occasionally the pilot has had to go around a storm; however, since we boarded the plane with the understanding we would be landing in Dallas, I have never left an airport not knowing to where we were going. With meticulous notes and flight logs, the pilot is aware of where he or she is taking the plane before they ever board.

Could you imagine what it would be like to get on an airplane and the pilot come over the intercom and say he has no clue where he's going? "I don't know where we're going, and we'll get there when we'll get there," he casually declares. If you were on that plane you might say, "Whoa, wait just a second!" And the person beside you says, "This ought to be fun!" If this ever happened to me while on a plane, I'm getting off that airplane because I want to know that the man in charge knows where we're going and how to get there.

It's the same concept when it comes to building a house. Blueprints are drawn by architects and engineers on purpose so that the house has the correct structure. There is purpose and intentionality applied so that the house has structural integrity. Plus, when you agreed to purchase a house that has three bedrooms, you don't want to end up with only one. When you thought you were getting two bathrooms, you don't end up with one and a half or one and an outhouse, right? The idea is this: The blueprint is supposed to direct the course of the building.

For our purpose, this same idea should be applied to parenting. As you think about parenting through the digital age, I want you to understand that you cannot approach it with a laziness or the philosophy of the pilot who says, "We'll end up where we end up!" or even the idea of "Well, I'll just deal with things as they come along." Truth be told, there are always going to be moments where you must deal with things as they come along, but in the grand scheme of things, if you are going to parent faithfully during the digital age, we must be intentional and deliberate. You won't accidentally end at the destination you want for your family. The destination you desire is only going to be reached because you were intentional.

Purpose in Your Mind

As the Old Testament book of Daniel opens, we learn of Nebuchadnezzar, the king of Babylon, besieging Jerusalem in the third year of the reign of king Jehoiakim (Daniel 1:1). This event, which historians believe took place around 605 B.C., is recorded in 2 Kings 24:1 when we read, *"In his days Nebuchadnezzar king of Babylon came up, and Jehoiakim became his servant for three years; then he turned and rebelled against him."* We also see this siege mentioned in 2 Chronicles 36:6-7 when we read, *"Nebuchadnezzar king of Babylon came up against him and bound him with bronze chains to take him to Babylon. Nebuchadnezzar also brought some of the articles of the house of the Lord to Babylon and put them in his temple at Babylon."* As part of this siege, we learn that *"some of the sons of Israel, including some of the royal family and of the nobles"* (Daniel 1:3) were also brought to Babylon and chosen to serve in the king's court. There are four young men who are specifically mentioned in Daniel 1:7 who serve as wonderful examples of conviction and commitment to God amongst a pagan culture: Daniel, Hananiah, Mishael, and Azariah. While all of these men serve as wonderful examples of conviction and commitment, I ask you to focus in on Daniel in chapter 1 verse 8, *"But Daniel made up his mind that he would not defile himself with the king's choice food or with the wine which he drank…."*

Being carted off into Babylonian captivity meant Daniel was forced to leave behind everything familiar to his childhood. In this new reality, the prisoners were expected to act a certain way that often was not honoring to God. What is so fascinating is that in this new culture, Daniel still had in his mind and his heart a strong dedication to God which compelled him to refuse the king's choice food and wine. It's so intriguing because the children of God were taken into captivity because of their disobedience to God. However, in the midst of this negative description, we find a young man (and his three friends!) who still remembered that Jehovah God is the only God.

How does this happen? How does Daniel reach the point where his conviction drove him to purpose in his heart or make up his mind not to defile himself? While I'm not certain we can pinpoint the exact reason, one component of the answer that is extremely reasonable is that his parents must have taught him to honor God. Daniel intentionally purposed that he wasn't going to allow the king's new culture—the feast, the food, the gods, the renaming away from his Hebrew name—to change him. That didn't happen because Daniel just woke up one day with indifference. He didn't reach this conviction by thinking to himself, "I'm just going to kind of see how it goes, kind of go with the flow." No, Daniel set his mind. And when he set his mind, then he was able to remain steadfast under extreme pressure.

It's this example of determination and clarity I want to use to illustrate what it takes to end at the destination every Christian parent wants for their child. Parenting faithfully is about identifying the destination; however, it's also about understanding and accepting the steadfast focus required along the way. If the mission is not properly defined and relayed to your family, they won't know where their going. If the mission doesn't remain in focus, giving up is a real possibility along the way. You and I will parent much more faithfully during this digital age when we set our minds to the course that God has for us and our children.

Keeping the Main Thing, the Main Thing

Why is it that we set rules for our children? Why do we establish limitations? Why is it that we talk to our children about certain subjects that are potential pitfalls? It's not because we're mean parents who want to make sure our children are raised in the absence of fun—contrary to what they might believe. It's because we understand what's at stake. We see things maybe that they can't see because we have different perspectives. We've walked a few miles in this journey of life. We know the highs of successes and the lows of failures. We've also learned the value of keeping our priorities straight and keeping our focus. However, sometimes we ourselves must be reminded of the extreme importance of priorities and focus in helping our children reach the desired destination—Heaven.

The greatest example we have of proper priorities and a keen focus is Jesus Christ. He unmistakably understood His purpose, and He stayed on point throughout His entire life on this earth. Scripture such as John 4:34 clearly state this, where Jesus said, *"My food is to do the will of Him who sent Me and to accomplish His work."* Or turn over to John 6:38, we again read of such focus when Jesus said, *"For I have come down from Heaven not to do My own will, but the will of Him who sent Me."* If we look at John 18:37, we find a similar passage where Pilate is speaking to Jesus and says, *"So you are a king. And Jesus answered, 'You say correctly that I am a king; for this I have been born and for this I have come into the world, to testify to the truth.'"*

Why did He come? To testify to the truth. He came to do the will of the Father. His food was never to do His own will but to do the will of the Father. There are over 30 statements in the New Testament that explicitly state why Jesus came to this world. While we know general statements about the reason Jesus came to this earth, such as John 3:16, it is also very telling to consider the idea that the Bible gives explicit statements regarding why Jesus came.

In the book of Matthew we read of five different reasons Jesus came to the earth that ultimately are the same concept but each approach the concept from different angles. Through this we learn Jesus was, speaking respectfully, the hunting dog who was locked in. He knew exactly what His goal was, and He did not veer from the goal. That's why He serves as our ultimate example in approaching our parenting with purposed, intentional, and deliberate focus.

Consider the following passages regarding the purpose of Jesus' coming to this earth from the book of Matthew:

- **Matthew 5:17** - *"Do not think that I came to abolish the Law or the Prophets;* ***I did not come to abolish but to fulfill****"* (emp. added).

- **Matthew 9:9-13** – *"As Jesus went on from there, He saw a man called Matthew, sitting in the tax collector's booth; and He said to him, 'Follow Me!' And he got up and followed Him. Then it happened that as Jesus was reclining at the table in the house, behold, many tax collectors and sinners came and were dining with Jesus and His disciples. When the Pharisees saw this, they said to His disciples, 'Why is your Teacher eating with the tax collectors and sinners?' But when Jesus heard this, He said, 'It is not those who are healthy who need a physician, but those who are sick. But go and learn what this means: 'I desire compassion, and not sacrifice,'* ***for I did not come to call the righteous, but sinners****"* (emp. added).

- **Matthew 10:34** - *"Do not think that I came to bring peace on the earth;* ***I did not come to bring peace, but a sword****"* (emp. added).

- **Matthew 18:11** – *"For the Son of Man has come* ***to save that which was lost****"* (emp. added).

- **Matthew 20:26-28** – *"It is not this way among you, but whoever wishes to become great among you shall be your servant, and whoever wishes to be first among you shall be your slave; just as the Son of Man did not come to be served, but* ***to serve, and to give His life a ransom for many****"* (emp. added).

When you and I read about the life and ministry of Jesus, we realize He knew exactly why He was here. He knew what He was supposed to be about, and He sought with everything in His life to accomplish that mission. That's why Jesus Christ serves as the greatest example of intentionality. His focus and dedication are the epitome of what it means to be deliberate. His example is filled with purpose. Just as He chose to be on point, we need to be laser focused as parents. How can we do that? How do we set out to accomplish parenting faithfully?

Developing a Family Mission Statement:

I want to show you how I evaluate where my family is going. We have done this with our children, and we've taught other parents to do the same. What is a family mission statement? Basically, it's a simple written statement that serves as a continual focus to help our family reach the goal. What goal? The obvious answer is that the goal is Heaven. While that's correct, we should understand that if we leave the goal so generic, we will miss a tremendous part of why we are here as disciples of Jesus Christ. In other words, if Heaven is the goal, what do I want my family to be doing in our time on this earth before we graduate into eternity?

As a word of caution, I ask you to consider the following. If we teach our children that the only reason they obey God is because at the end they will get something out of it, is that not a selfish-driven religion? Is that not emphasizing selfishness? In other words, take away Heaven. Would you still obey God? I offer this for your consideration because we've got to be cautious about teaching our children that the sole reason we obey God is because we get something out of doing so. Personally, we have taught our children that our number one goal as a family is to go to Heaven. Our number two goal is to take as many people there with us as possible. So I'm not in any way, shape, or form saying that

Heaven can't be a major emphasis and major goal. However, as we consider family mission statements, I want you also to be thinking about what your family goals need to be while still here on the earth.

When developing a family mission plan, we must begin by asking, **What is the dream that you have for your family?** If you could plan out the careers of your children, what would you put on the discussion table? What do you really want for your children? Chances are most of you would say, "I want them to be successful," or "I want them to have a job where they can take care of their family." You may say your wish for your children would be that they work at a place surrounded by people who appreciate them. What about when it comes to their intellect, their education? What about their emotional well-being? What about their social well-being? What about their future families? If you could dream about all those things, what would you say? What if I asked you about your dreams for your family spiritually, what would you say? If I challenged you even further and listed all of these things out on a piece of paper, personal growth, career, intellect, emotional, social, physical, family, and then I put spiritual on there as well, which one would you circle as the number one most important goal for your children?

I take for granted, since you are engaging in this study, that your answer would be the spiritual component of your children is most significant. That's because you understand something very important. You understand that one day they're going to leave their job, and someone else will sit in that chair, be it from retirement or from death. You understand that no matter how much education they get and no matter how good their grades are, that when they stand before God Almighty, He's not going to ask, "Did you get *As* or did you get *Cs*?" Because in eternity it won't matter. Whether they were liked or not liked socially won't matter in eternity. "Did they rise on the corporate ladder?" is an insignificant question when eternity is the perspective you use to evaluate their lives. You already know that the only thing that matters is their standing before God. So, since that's the only thing that ultimately matters, we must think about who they are while they live in this world.

I want you to think about Hebrews 11:16. As I grow, I want this in my own life and I want this for our children as well. Hebrews 11:16 says, *"But as it is, they desire a better country, that is, a heavenly one; therefore God is not ashamed to be called their God."* If there is anything said about me, I want this to be said. God is not ashamed to be called my God. I want Him to say that about our children, and I want Him to say that about my wife Erin. I want God to say, "Yes, I am their God, and I'm proud that I'm their God."

My question is, "Why did God say that about the people in Hebrews 11?" Was it because they were perfect and had no sin? No. It's because they continued to put their faith and trust in God, and their faith was not merely a mental exercise. In every person in Hebrews 11, you see a conviction aligned with action. In other words, their steps were in line with their beliefs. Their beliefs were merely empty words. They weren't pew warmers and merely "church attenders." Their steps were motivated by faith, and God said that He was not ashamed to be called their God.

Consider also Romans 12:1-2. It's a passage you may know very well. This is also something I want for my family. *"Therefore I urge you, brethren, by the mercies of God to present your bodies a living and holy sacrifice, acceptable to God, which is your spiritual service of worship; and do not be conformed to this world, but be transformed by the renewing of your mind."* I want my children to be transformed. You know *transformed* is literally the word from which we get our word metamorphosis. Metamorphosis, for example, is a caterpillar turning into a butterfly. Scripture says transformation is supposed to be an intentional part of the life of all disciples of Jesus. We are not to be conformed to this world. We are not to align ourselves or be made in the mold of this world. We are to be the caterpillar that turns into a butterfly in the transformation, the metamorphosis of your mind. And in so doing, we prove the will of God is good. I want that to be said for myself and my children.

Other Scriptures we considered in our family mission statement are:

- **2 Corinthians 5:1**—*"For we know that if the earthly tent which is our house is torn down, we have a building from God, a house not made with hands, eternal in the heavens."*
    - o I want my family to desire the eternal house not made with hands.

- **1 Peter 1:3-4**—*"Blessed be the God and Father of our Lord Jesus Christ, who according to His great mercy has caused us to be born again to a living hope through the resurrection of Jesus Christ from the dead, to obtain an inheritance which is imperishable and undefiled and will not fade away, reserved in heaven for you...."*
    - o I want our family to inherit the incorruptible, undefiled prize—the reward that is in Heaven.

- **Matthew 5:13-16**—*"You are the salt of the earth; but if the salt has become tasteless, how can it be made salty again? It is no longer good for anything, except to be thrown out and trampled underfoot by men. You are the light of the world. A city set on a hill cannot be hidden; nor does anyone light a lamp and put it under a basket, but on the lampstand, and it gives light to all who are in the house. Let your light shine before men in such a way that they may see your good works, and glorify your Father who is in Heaven."*
    - o I understand that we are salt and light, and as we live in this world, I want our lives to bring glory to God.

- **Matthew 22:37**—*"And He said to him, 'You shall love the Lord your God with all your heart, and with all your soul, and with all your mind.' This* *is the great and foremost commandment. The second is like it, 'You shall love your neighbor as yourself.'"*

       o I want our family to love God with everything that we are and love others in a manner that glorifies God.

If that's what I want, there's got to be a transition from thinking "I want that" to "How do I make that happen?" If this transition doesn't occur, any dream we have will just stay as a hypothetical theory. If the dream and idea is never condensed and communicated in a way that our children can grasp and make personal in their lives, then all they're going to think is, "Well, that's just Dad. That's what he wants." If they never see steps being taken to make the plan a reality, they may think to themselves, "Dad talks about that, but I see what we're doing and it's not lining up." One of the most humbling things as a parent is for your children to hear what you want and then see how often you fail. That's why I also want our children to know that repentance, grace, and mercy are a big part of this statement and plan. I want them to know there is a way back to God, and that way is through Jesus Christ.

The challenge with the mission is to bring the dream and vision down to some key words and some tangible concepts that can start being fleshed out in manageable and measurable ways. We don't want the mission to be like the business team that sits around a table and says, "Okay, what's our goal for this year?", and somebody speaks up saying, "To bring in more money!" And they all just look at each other and think, "But how are we going to do that?" It's this "How are we going to do that?" question that people often skip in the plan. When they do, the team is left with an idea but no way to accomplish the idea. The same is true when the family mission is left in the general category. Children are left with a major dilemma saying to themselves, "Well, I know my mom and dad want me to go to Heaven, but I don't know how that's going to look." They may think, "I know they want me to say that God's not ashamed to be my God and they want me to bring glory and honor to God, but how is all that going to happen?" And that's where it gets down to the measurable component of the family mission statement. The measurable component has tangibles. It must have specifics, it must be measurable, it must have time limits, it must be personally accepted, and it must be in writing.

Five Components of Goal Setting

These five key components of reaching goals do not come from my own thoughts; they are researched and tested necessities of reaching goals.[3] So, let's seriously consider steps that will help make your dream for your family a tangible and workable plan.

Step #1: They must be specific. It's not enough to say my goal is to lose weight. I must say a specific amount of weight—my goal is to lose 30 pounds. That's easy, you say, because you can lose 30 pounds over 10 years, right? That brings us to step 2!

Step #2: It must be limited in time. My goal is to lose 30 pounds in the year 2024. Now you have set a specific goal in a specific time. Next you need to decide how you will measure success along the way.

Step #3: It must be measurable. For example, I'm going to measure success by saying 30 pounds over 12 months means less than 3 pounds a month. Therefore, my goal is to lose 3 pounds a month.

Step #4: It must be put into writing. Why would I put it in writing? And why would I tack that up say to a refrigerator door? Because when I go to grab the chocolate cake, I might ask how does this help me reach my 3 pounds this month?

Step #5: It must be personally accepted by all. The goals must be personally accepted by everyone in the family. It's not enough, parents, for you to say, "I want my children to go to Heaven." They must want to go to Heaven. Otherwise, they're just doing what somebody else wants. And at the end of the day, guess what? It wasn't personally accepted as their plan, so therefore, they have no reason to want to accomplish it.

The Roman philosopher Seneca once said, "If a man knows not to which port he sails, no wind is favorable."[4] I've also heard that when you don't know where you're going, you will always end up there. Parents, what I want you to hear is this: when it comes to the spiritual well-being of your homes-when it comes to parenting with purpose-it is an intentional, deliberate, and purposeful endeavor. It's something that you've communicated to your families, you've discussed with your families, and that your family has personalized in their own lives. The goal is not their obedience; the goal is their hearts.

Understanding Different Parenting Styles

Psychologists and those who study families and parenting tell us there are four different types of parenting styles. The four different parenting styles are indulgent, authoritarian, authoritative, and uninvolved. You may find yourself in one single category; however, like me, you may see yourself in multiple categories. Either way, it's important to evaluate your parenting style as you consider the question of "How do I go about winning the hearts of my children to the Lord?"

Let's just go ahead and get this one out of the way. The uninvolved parent is not a good parenting style. This is the parent who doesn't care and is permissive. This parent says, "Oh, kids will just be kids. I'm not going to make any demands on them." Maybe it's the great grandmother or the grandmother who has been there, done that, and they're tired. "Oh, just let them. Who cares? It's only four pieces of chocolate cake. And they only get to do it when they're at my house. It's okay." Then the parent comes in and says, "What are you doing? I told them no." The parent who is permissive or uninvolved is one who's low in responsiveness to their children, but they also are low in demanding. In other words, they just let them do whatever.

Children who grow up with parents like this typically have low self-esteem. They have very little confidence, and they may seek inappropriate substitutes for their parents. In other words, if you don't parent them, then they will seek someone else whom they can latch onto. And that's not always a brother or sister in Christ. Usually they are left confused asking, "Why did my parents not care enough to parent me?" or "What makes them want to be uninvolved in my life?" These children usually walk away with extremely low self-esteem.

The next style to consider is the authoritarian parenting style. The authoritarian style is highly demanding and not very responsive. They are obedience driven and status oriented. It's not that they don't care about the kids; they just care about not looking like bad parents in front of people.

You may have grown up with this style of parenting. I know I was told this phrase sometimes: "Children are to be seen and not heard." That philosophy is an authoritarian approach to parenting. In other words, "You will not embarrass me. You sit down, you will be quiet until you're spoken to. You will do what I say because I've said it."

Do I think that there's some validity to some of that? Yes, because kids don't always need to know why. They need to know the authority figure in their life told them to do something, and they, as children, need to be obedient. God's Word states this in Ephesians 6:1, "Children, obey your parents in the Lord, for this is right." I can't think of a time when a child's obedience to parents is dependent on a great explanation from the parent to the child. Some would say once a parent explains why, then the child should submit. However, the Bible makes it clear that children are to submit to their parents.

Children need to learn this important lesson early in life. When they get their first job and the boss tells them to do something, they can't turn around and say, "Well, my parents always told me that I could ask why, so do you mind if I ask why?" That boss is going to say, "I don't owe you an answer, and if you don't do what I tell you, you can leave." The police officer is not always going to give a why. The truth is, God doesn't always give a why. Do I believe there's some validity to this style of parenting? Yes—typically the child raised by an authoritarian style of parenting performs moderately well in school, and they're not involved in problem behavior. However, studies show that they also have poor social skills, low self-esteem, and higher levels of depression. So let's consider another style.

The authoritative parenting style is demanding and responsive. However, they are also very high in responsiveness to the child. In other words, they try to live a balanced approach. They have expectations, but they also want the children to personalize the rules. They will take time to explain the reasoning behind the rule when appropriate. They will not entertain disobedience or strong-willed arguing, and they must know the difference between a genuine question for understanding and an accumulation of ammunition for debate. That means the authoritative parent must take the time to learn about their children. They must study their individual personalities and respond appropriately to each individual child. The authoritative parent explains rules, discusses, and is supportive, and—probably the biggest difference—they listen to the child's viewpoint. Now, I didn't say they do what the child wants. But they do listen to the child's viewpoint.

To better illustrate the importance of this parenting style, imagine your job requires you to work as part of a team. As the team comes together and brainstorms ideas and methods of approach, you offer your opinion and expertise. However, none of your other co-workers ever wants to hear what you think. How much a part of the team do you feel? Your point of view is consistently passed over as being meaningless. How does that make you feel? How would you approach the team and working together? How would you approach your task? If you don't feel appreciated, then you will begin to speak up less and withdraw. You may even begin to check out and look for another job. Children at times—teenagers especially—report feeling the same way as you would. They feel pushed away not because Mom and Dad didn't do everything the teen said, but because they didn't even take the time to listen what their teen had to say.

That's a big deal that we as adults need to understand: In parenting faithfully, it's not just us making demands—it's us trying to win the hearts of our children. Because we're playing what I call "the long game." That means, we are not short sighted in our mission. We know Heaven is the goal, and we want everything we do to be pointed at the main target. The long game says if my child grows up and is at the church building every time the doors are open because I said they had to be and never because they wanted to be, then what's going to happen when they leave my house and are on their own? It's the same with devices. Say I have a bunch of rules for television or the internet or video gaming or on their cell phones. They abide by what I say while they're in my home. However, the only reason they're doing it is I told them to. When they leave my house, what might happen? They may rebel because it was never personal to them. Their heart was never won. The goal of parenting faithfully in a digital age is Heaven. That's where we want our children to be. But at the core we must win and protect the hearts of our kids.

2

Growing Up Connected

Think for a moment about Lego blocks. Most of us are familiar with these; many have had the unpleasant experience of stepping on one. While I don't know all the history behind the creation of Lego and their design, I can imagine someone, at some point, stacking blocks and thinking, "What if we add pegs on one and holes on another so they could interlock and stay together?" Probably an interesting story. What I do know is this: a single Lego doesn't accomplish much. It might look impressive sitting on a table or a shelf, but in terms of purpose, it remains unfulfilled. The true power of a Lego comes to life when it's connected to others—because that's what it was designed to do. Legos are meant to be part of something larger, and it's through their connections that they realize their purpose.

I am truly mesmerized by what people can accomplish with Legos. In fact, I've learned that there are actually jobs where individuals build with Lego blocks full-time. If you've ever seen those life-size or even larger-than-life figures, you can't help but stop and marvel at them. Imagine the patience and precision it takes to connect one small Lego to another, piece by piece, until a complex figure or scene comes to life. Personally, I'd probably reach a point where, after placing a couple thousand pieces, I'd realize I made a mistake 1,000 pieces ago, forcing me to go back and tear everything apart. But even with the challenges, I'm always drawn to what people can create. The lesson? When things meant to be connected come together in the right way, incredible things can happen. Beautiful images and impressive creations emerge when each piece is placed with intention and purpose.

When you and I reflect on the way we are created by God, we are like these Legos. If I were alone on a deserted island, could I still worship God by myself? Yes, I could. Could I praise God by myself? Yes. However, something will always be missing if it's just me and no one else. You can look through the Bible and see times when prophets felt like they were the only ones left. Elijah thought that no one else alive was going to help him, and God came to him in a whirlwind and told him that there were others who had not bowed a knee. Consider Adam in the garden in Genesis 2:18—the very first time God said something wasn't good was about man being alone. Or in Joshua 1 when Moses died and Joshua was called into leadership, God told him on three separate occasions: *"Be strong and courageous"* (1:6, 7, 9). But verse 9 emphasizes the sense of connectedness. The Bible says, *"Have I not commanded you? Be strong and courageous, and do not tremble or be dismayed, for the Lord your God is with you wherever you go."*

Jesus promises to be with us. He said that to His disciples. What does a person gain by knowing that they are not alone, by knowing there's a sense of needing to be connected? For Joshua, he understood that no matter what battle he fought, no matter what enemy he engaged, God was with him, and therefore all would be okay. God was going to win those battles. All Joshua had to do was be strong and courageous and walk where God said walk and stop where God said stop, and God was going to be with him.

For Adam, it's something different. God was also going to be with him; however, something was missing in his life, and Adam didn't even know what. God looked down and said it's not good for man to be alone. God is the one who said it's not good for man to be alone. In other words, He created us with a need to be connected.

Since 2020, many slogans and phrases have come about that truly have gone against and have worked against the concept that we are created with a need to be connected, how we are connected, and what connected really means. Things like social distance or staying 6 feet away. Those slogans became all too common during Covid. Individuals truly did suffer because of not being connected. For example, nursing home visits ceased or became very limited. I read stories regarding individuals in their 80s who went into nursing homes just before the Coronavirus hit and before the nursing homes were locked down. Throughout the months, individuals who had a full vocabulary went to hardly speaking. In our own family, my grandmother was in a nursing home in Texas, where they totally cut off individuals from being able to go in. My uncle, who lived there, and his family could look and visit through the window because she could not even get out of her house. She died during the Coronavirus shutdown. What happened in many homes or nursing homes went against our need for connection, the benefit of human touch, the benefit of conversation, and the benefit of being together.

I have spoken with numerous elderships since 2020 regarding the impact of the pandemic and the shutdown that was included. Nothing like that had ever happened in our lifetime where we could say, "Oh, I remember when this occurred back here, and this is what the elders did." That didn't happen. The elders tried to navigate a challenging situation. Some members never came back. The concern elders feel about this has been verbalized to me numerous times because we've slipped into thinking that there's a substitute for what God intended regarding the church and our worshipping Him. You see, the church, at its very core, is to glorify God. You can do that on your own in your own house. However, if that is all the gathering of the saints is about, why in God's wisdom did He say to come together into a body called a family, a household? It's because the need for connection is very real among humanity, including Christians.

Generational Considerations

As we begin this discussion, we need to understand that the generation people are in affect how they define our times. When considering generational studies, we should ask, "Why are people coming from where they are?" Cultural research entities such as the Pew Research Forum have a breakdown of the generations in America up to Generation Z, those born between 1997 and 2012. I'm sure you've heard some mention the newest generation, Generation Alpha—those born since 2012. This generation is still so young and developing that many who study generational trends and markers haven't identified strong descriptions other than they believe Alpha children are the offspring of very young Generation X and mainly Millennials.

Understanding the generations alive today is not just a matter of historical interest but also a key to understanding the society we live in. It provides insights into the values, beliefs, and behaviors that shape our world. This is why it's important to consider the generations alive today.

Including Gen Alpha, there are seven generations of individuals alive today. We must consider what has shaped each generation. A few of these generational markers include:

- Being very young children during World War I
- Fighting in World War II
- Communism's threat to democracy
- The race to outer space

- The Cold War
- The Vietnam War
- The Korean War
- The Gulf War
- The Hippie, or free love, movement
- More mothers working outside of the home
- The creation of latchkey kids
- The World Trade Towers being bombed
- The War on Terror
- Afghanistan
- Covid-19
- ...And so many more

These are all vital markers in generational studies.

Today, generations are often labeled based on aspects related to the digital world. The most common name for today's teenagers is Generation Z. However, there is another individual who has significantly contributed to the study of generational differences. Her work is considered a standard in understanding the younger generations. Her name is Jean Twenge, and she has termed the teenage generation the "iGen generation." Her markers are based upon technological advances over time, providing a fascinating insight into the changes that have occurred over the years.

The Need to Connect

Now, before we move too far into this chapter, please understand that the need to communicate and connect has always been there. We're not talking about the core concepts that haven't been a part of generations of the past. Whether the telegraph, the telephone, handwritten letters, postcards, gathering in community spaces like a ballpark or town square, or newspapers and getting the day's news from the boys selling the papers, mankind has always desired to connect and communicate with one another. The difference is, today the mediums have changed. The desire has stayed the same, but how we connect and communicate has changed. Today it is video chats, social media, video games, or texting—all of those are about connection and communicating with one another. These changes have not only revolutionized the way we interact but have also significantly impacted various aspects of our society, from business and politics to culture and personal relationships.

Before we look at what's going on today and say, "It's just all bad," or "I can't believe where we're at today," we just need to think—is it possible that the way we look at the digital age is based upon the generation we are? Could we be skewed slightly to say, "Well, then all those new-fangled things, I didn't grow up with that; kids don't need that today?" At the core, it's the same desire as when you were children. That is—I want to connect with people, I want to communicate with people, and they want to communicate and connect with me. The only difference is the medium. Your perspective, shaped by your experiences and the era you grew up in, plays a significant role in how you perceive modern communication. So we must remember that as technology continues to change, so does the way to communicate and connect.

Timeline of Technological Advancements

In 1995, the internet was commercialized and made available to average households. In 1997, the first social media sites appeared. Probably you didn't know about any of those. Chances are the first social media sites that many of us ever heard of was My Space in 2003. Facebook first opened to everyone above the age of 13 in 2006. In 2007, the first iPhone was introduced, and in 2010 the first iPad. We must consider that when people study facts and the impact massive changes have on society, they follow the effects and impact for years. But 2007 was not that long ago, so the long-term effect of these technological changes is not yet completely understood and the impacts studied. We're talking about how quickly things have changed in a 25-year period.

If you are from one of the older generations, which we define as those who were born before the digital revolution, the speed of the technological changes may seem to be so fast that you feel left behind. If that's the way you feel, it's understandable. However, for many young parents today, you're a part of the generations that have grown up with technology, and all you've known is where we are today. We need to remember that those born after 2007 don't know what it was like before the iPhone or the iPad.

If you feel you're getting left behind by the rapidly changing digital landscape, you can't just throw your hands up in frustration. Remember what we talked about in the first chapter? We've got to be deliberate, intentional, and purposed. If we're going to do that, we cannot fall asleep. You know when you get to sleep? When you die. And then it's a great sleep because it's a sleep from the wiles of Satan and from the work; it's a beautiful rest.

How Connected Are We?

How connected are we today? Research shows that, on average, for children 0 to 8 years old:

- they spend 2.5 hours in front of a screen daily
- 5 to 8-year-olds spend three hours on screens every day
- 39 minutes a day of online video viewing dominated the kids' screen time, and most of that through streaming services or on YouTube

- Nearly 50 percent of 2 to 4-year-olds have their own tablet (Who's buying the tablet for them? Perhaps they get the hand-me-downs?)
- 67 percent of 5 to 8-year-olds have their own tablet[1]

The majority of parents of children this age has a positive view of the amount of time their children spend on the screen. Why are they are so happy? Most parents are okay with the amount of time their children spend on devices because it means that they don't have to entertain the child. Be honest. I know it's really easy to hand children a device and allow them to be entertained so that I can focus on my day. Anybody who says that they've never done that, I'm not sure I trust you, because it happens before you know it. Next time you're out at a restaurant, I challenge you to look around and see how many children are on a device.

As children age from 5 to 8, their media usage becomes more independent. This shift means that parents are not as engaged with their children when it comes to media as much between the ages of 5 and 8 compared to when they're 0 to 4. In other words, the momma or the daddy tends to sit there with a child 0 to 4 years old. By age 5 to 8, the parents tend to hand them the device and let them go off and do their own thing. However, this independence also brings potential risks that parents must be aware of and manage.

Regarding children ages 9 to 12, survey data suggests that 42% of U.S. kids have a phone by age 10. By age 14, smartphone ownership climbs to 91%.[2] Also, studies show that 68% in this category have a social media account.[3] Children age 9 to 12 years old are called tweens, so some fall on the top end of what I just told you about 5 to 8-year-olds, and some fall on the bottom end of what I'm about to tell you with teenagers. But the big thing that I want you to remember is that social media sites, for the longest time, required that you had to be 13 years of age or older to have a social media account. However, we now see many young people who are younger than 13 have social media accounts. Is it because their parents let them? Maybe not directly let them. Here's why—if media usage becomes more independent between the ages of 5 and 8, why would media usage become more dependent between the ages of 9 and 12? In other words, why would I assume that moms and dads are more concerned about spending time with their children on media between 9 and 12 than they are when they are under 8?

Here's a possibility as to why preteens have social media accounts. Is it possible parents have become so detached that they don't know what their 10- to 12-year-olds are doing on the internet? All the 10- to 12-year-olds have to do is go on that social media site, click a button that says they are a certain age, put in a fake birthday, and the website accepts it. It's that easy for a child who's underage to have a social media site. Another reason for early use of social media accounts by preteens is because parents feel the social media site standard should not be the standard for their own family standard. In other words, if say Facebook requires you to be 13 to have an account, the parent can say, "Well, you're 11; I think as long as you only interact with your grandma and grandpa and aunts and uncles and your brothers and sisters and your mom and dad, it's fine." Or they may say, "Well, the social media company says 13, but we believe 10 is fine." Or maybe the parent says, "Oh, who cares? Go ahead and do whatever you want. Mess up your own life if you want to mess it up." One of those three has to happen because otherwise, there's no way a child under 13 can set up their own account without one of those three occurring.

When it comes to teenagers, how connected are they?

- Teenagers spend, on average, 9 hours per day on screens for entertainment, not including what they spend on devices for school related activities and work.[4]

- When you couple that with 17 hours a day spent in school, sleeping, homework, or school activities, it looks like they have more time than they should. 17 plus 9 equals 26. How do they get those two extra hours? The good news is they have the same time as you and I. They just usually multi-task and engage in multiple forms of screen usage at the same time. They may have a show streaming while engaging with friends on a social media site and texting someone simultaneously.
- Also, just food for thought: If a person were only to spend an average of 50 hours per week on devices from ages 13 to 18—that's equivalent to more than 12 school years!
- They spend 4.8 hours per day using social media apps[5]
- On average, teens receive 237 notifications every day[6]
- 46% say they are almost constantly online[7]
- Teens spend on average 2.25 hours per day texting[8]

Now, these statistics were not significantly different when considering junior high students. There was a little decrease in texting and online usage, but gaming and video chat were the same. Understand, showing you these statistics isn't a declaration of right or wrong. I want you to see how connected this generation, Generation Z, and the newest one, Generation Alpha, is because that plays into parenting. There are benefits to being connected, but there are also negative effects because they're so connected. I'm not just talking about some of the obvious—it also includes the psychological and emotional well-being of our children. Self-esteem is impacted. There are a lot of different impacts, much less some of the stuff we will cover, such as sexually explicit material, child predators, or cyberbullying.

The research continues to say:

- Young people watch 2.6 hours of TV daily, and most are not watched on flatscreens hanging on the wall but on cell phones [9]

- 97% of teens use social media every day[10]
- 85% of U.S. teens report playing video games, and 41% say they play them at least once a day
- The average time spent on video games every day is 1.5 hours[11]

Gaming has an element of chat. So, within gaming, it's not just that they're on their PlayStation or their Xbox playing a game; it's that they're on and talking to other people, reading what other people are saying. Ask yourself—do we know these other people, and what they are saying?

Regarding social media, Snapchat, Instagram, and TikTok are very familiar to today's teens. Facebook has taken a severe dive among young people.[12] That should not surprise us. Typically, young people don't like to hang out where older people are hanging out, and older people took over Facebook. Older people are starting to take over Instagram, at least to an extent.

Regarding teenagers and smartphone ownership, research shows that 95% of today's teens have access to a smartphone.[13] Many parents today can still remember when mobile phones came out. I remember my dad carrying a bag phone, and I know there were some phones before that. They were bricks. We remember what it was to talk on the phone when the cord would stretch across the kitchen. Remember that first time you had a cordless phone and how much freedom that was? Then cell phones came out, and they were so expensive that nobody could afford them. I remember my first one was only an emergency-use cell phone because the minutes cost so much. Remember flip phones? To text on those early flip phones you had to push the button three times to get the letter you wanted. Then you waited a second, the cursor moved over, then you pressed the button two times to get that letter, and then it moved over again.

Kids today have thumbs that seem so conditioned to texting that some can do this quicker than they can talk because they've become so accustomed to that form of communication. Smartphones have replaced flip phones. Phones aren't used to talk anymore. As a matter of fact, if you're a grandparent and are curious why your grandchildren never call you, don't worry. They don't call anybody. If you want to talk to your grandchildren, you need to learn how to text or be on social media because that's where you're more likely to communicate with them.

Screen Time Recommendations[14]

The American Academy of Pediatrics makes recommendations about how much screen time children should have. Please consider the media time usage you see in young people today. They recommend for birth to 18 months no screen time. Their research has shown lasting adverse effects at this age on children's language development, reading ability, and short-term memory. The earlier they are exposed to screen time, the lower their reading skills, the lower their short-term memory, and the lower their development of language skills. Studies have shown problems associated with sleep and attention can exist as well. However, it was interesting that the American Academy of Pediatrics said chatting with your grandparents between 0 and 18 months over video conferencing is okay. Babies do not communicate in the same way that teenagers do. They respond to facial expressions and noises. The time spent video conferencing with the grandparents is not necessarily shunned because it still has a component of facial expression. Therefore the part of the 0- to 18-month-old's brain that is geared to respond can still be appropriately stimulated.

The American Academy of Pediatrics recommends that children aged 18 months to 2 years have no more than 15 minutes of screen time daily. Did you hear that? Up to 2 years, the American Academy of Pediatrics recommends no more than 15 minutes a day. They say that 15 minutes needs to be "high quality" children's media. High-quality children's media is not *Sponge Bob SquarePants* or the cartoons you and I grew up on. *Popeye, Roadrunner,* and *Bugs Bunny* do not count as high quality media. The old Mickey Mouse and Donald Duck cartoons are not in the high-quality category either.

"High-quality" children's media would include things like *Daniel Tiger's Neighborhood* or *Blue's Clues*. Think *Mr. Roger's Neighborhood* and *Sesame Street*. Any cartoon or show that falls in line with something that will get the child engaged and actively involved, is meaningful in its message, includes social interaction between other people, and also presents a learning goal would be included. I understand that many children want to laugh and have fun when it comes to screen time; however, the Academy has reasons to recommend no more than 15 minutes a day.

For the 2 to 5-year-olds, the American Academy of Pediatrics recommends no more than 1 hour a day of high-quality entertainment. They also say this should be less than an hour straight. Break it up into 15-minute segments throughout the day. That means you get four 15-minute segments or less because they want to stress the concept that you cannot replace other childhood experiences with being on media all the time. In other words, the brain develops better in young people when they are forced to play outside with other young people, converse, come up with a game and rules, then play and hold each other accountable according to those rules. The playing together, the building things—the Lego concept—all have to do with brain development. Parents and grandparents aren't just trying to be mean.

It's all about brain development. Remember the prefrontal cortex, which has to do with impulses, memory, and language skill sets, doesn't fully develop until age 25. And what we do from 0 to 25 can impact that development greatly—these are really crucial, critical years. This is not, "Well, what am I going to do?" The better question is, "How do I want my child to end up as an adult?" Because what you do now impacts the kind of adult they turn out to be.

In researching this topic, I read an article in *The New York Times* about people who work in Silicon Valley, where a lot of the technology is introduced. There is a growing trend among parents there to keep their children away from technology for as long as possible.[16] These are the people who create this stuff. That is something we need to think about.

For 6 to 12-year-olds, the research says to start small and work your way up. 30 minutes a day for a 6-year-old increasing each year up to 2 hours a day for a 12-year-old. Be aware this is when many of the schools start requiring more online work. The guidelines for 13 to 15-year-olds are from 2 hours a day to no more than 4 hours a day. That's total screen time. I told you before that most teenagers today spend 9 hours of time on the internet or on screens or in entertainment. Why do they do that? Here's why. Research shows that one to two hours of screen time per day is often associated with positive social-emotional behavior, with problems reported in some instances when the amount goes above four hours a day.[17] Social-emotional behavior is impacted by media usage. When you start to think about how much time teens spend and what they're doing, this is the age that most people are bullied for the first time online. The more time they spend, the more open they are to it.

I disagree with the American Academy of Pediatrics' recommendation for children 16+ years. The Academy says at that age you are transitioning in your parenting and become more of an advice-giving person and a context so that you want that open communication. Your teen says,

"Hey, I saw this the other day." You want that open communication with your teenager so they will allow you to talk with them through that. I'm all about open communication, but I don't think we should throw our hands up and say, "If you want to spend 12 hours a day on the internet, you go right ahead because the AAP says I shouldn't tell you not to." I still think there's value in setting limits.

Three Major Reasons to Pay Attention

There are at least three areas and three reasons that impact why our young people growing up connected ought to be something we think about. The first one is brain development, which has already been mentioned a couple of times. The prefrontal cortex is where executive functions occur. Executive functions include cognitive flexibility, working memory, and inhibitory control. In other words, this area of the brain makes us pause and consider the positives and negatives of decisions and behaviors. Since the prefrontal cortex is not fully developed until age 25, we can understand that anything that factors into this development or behaviors that stem from a lack of inhibitory functions operating at maximum capacity should be something to which we parents pay attention.

The executive function of cognitive flexibility allows all of us to consider alternative perspectives. It enables us to look at different perspectives and strategies, shift attention from one source to another, stay on point, solve problems, be creative, and think critically. That happens in the prefrontal cortex. Working memory is the ability to hold and mentally manipulate information in our minds so that we can bring that back out and use it later. This function allows children to do addition and subtraction, follow a story, and remember the rules of a game. Both cognitive flexibility and working memory are processed in the prefrontal cortex.

Inhibitory control is about controlling automatic and impulsive behaviors. This skill enables us to make choices and achieve goals by suppressing a dominant response or impulse to do something to achieve a goal as well as resist distraction. Have you ever noticed a child who has attention problems? That is because the prefrontal cortex is not firing on all cylinders. Studies have shown the more media, the more of an impact on impulse and attention. I believe that there are things such as ADD and ADHD. That's not a question. However, I think we need to consider possible factors that contribute to the problem. I know our diets have changed—we have more preservatives in our food today than in other generations, and we're learning that preservatives impact overall health. But we also have more media today. I don't think it's any coincidence that we see more cases of diagnosed ADD and ADHD today.

The question that arises is why? Did children not face difficulties in sitting still or paying attention before? The truth is yes, they did. However, as we allow technology and media to increasingly influence and shape children's brains, particularly at younger ages, it will continue to impact their emotional and social behavior. We need to be mindful of and cautious about this significant aspect.

Last, let's consider brain plasticity. The brain grows at the fastest point from 0 to 6 years of age and then again in the teen years. Imagine a concrete patio, a concrete step, or a steppingstone that hasn't solidified. You put your hands, or the hands of your little children, on it so that it will forever have their handprints solidified. You may even write their names or their initials beside their hands. You put a date in the concrete, and once it's solidified, it will be there forever—or at least until someone comes in and busts up the concrete. So it is with children's brains. The "concrete" of their brains is not set from 0 to 6 years of age and during the teen years. As we age, the "concrete" does, in fact, become set. However, that doesn't mean you and I can't continue to learn. We may not learn as quickly because we have impressions made in our minds that we may have to overcome. That's the point. Whatever impressions have been made in that concrete when we were young, it is more challenging to get them out when we are older. That's why what is allowed to make impressions between ages 0 to 6 and during the teen years is especially crucial for brain development.

Number two is the idea of friendships and relationships. As children age, especially during the teen years, they turn more to their peers. Turning to their peers should not hurt us because that's part of growing up—they become more aware of what other people think of them. They also want to connect with people outside their biological families. Many parents may feel like they're choosing other people over them. Well, the reality is you did the same thing. It's part of growing up, learning who you are and your identity, and learning how to function within a culture among other people. However, in today's digital age, these friendships are more likely to occur online first. That fact should scare us—that our children can count as a "friend" someone who they have never met and only talked to online—and is good reason to be unsettled.

In reality, for teenagers and younger children growing up today, very few see what happens in real life or the virtual world as any different. It's all one and the same. The reason it's one and the same is that those teenagers may only talk to each other during the day or at the lunchroom table, they may message each other on social media, and then they'll get home and get on video games. Then they'll talk to each other the whole night playing video games. And then they'll show up the next day, maybe they'll talk in person then about the video game and go about their daily life, and then they'll get online and talk. It's no different for them whether they speak to one another in person or message online. It's all the same. That's why face-to-face communication is not the number one preferred way to communicate for young people. Texting is, and if you want to communicate with kids today, you need to learn to text. If you're not on social media, you're missing out on your communication with your kids.

The next aspect of this one, which is incredibly concerning for many parents today, is the "romantic side." Ironically, it's not romance at all but the sending of inappropriate pictures or content online. This is called sexting and includes sending sexually explicit videos, images, or messages through text, direct messages, and online social media platforms.

- 1 in 7 teens say they have sent "sexts."
- 1 in 4 teens say they have received "sexts."
- 14.5% of "sexts" teens receive are forwarded to other people.[18]

With COVID-19 and school administrations' decisions across America to school at home, we discovered a severe uptick among young children and teenagers. Even knowing that passing along these images is the same as passing along child pornography and you can be arrested hasn't slowed it. The threat of spending time in jail or getting fined still hasn't stopped it. Why is that? Honestly, that's an entirely different subject and outside the scope of this book. But let's consider a couple of things.

Most of the young people who engage in this behavior do so for two main reasons—one, as a flirtatious behavior with someone they like or are in a dating relationship with. They want to show their commitment to that relationship as part of the flirtatiousness. That's an interesting way to think, isn't it? The other side of that is peer pressure. They are pressured by friends to participate in things. I've been speaking on this particular subject for many years. After one of my seminars, a fifth-grade teacher came up to me. She said, "Joe, you're right. This is not just a teenage thing. This is actually getting into elementary schools." She said that at her school, they found out that girls were asking to use the restroom, and while there, they were taking pictures of their upper body, and then they were sending it to boys at the high school. She said the kids considered it a game. If a person could guess whose picture it was, there was a "prize." You think, "Why would fifth graders—fifth grade!—do such a thing?" They're supposed to be playing and thinking about innocent things. Unfortunately, the more and more this behavior becomes normalized, the younger and younger we will see this happening. Does it matter how much time they spend on their phones and with social media? Does it matter what they're doing while on the video game and who they're communicating with? Absolutely it does. Whose job is it to make sure that they stay safe?

The last thing I want you to consider is *the impact digital technology has on the health of our children*. While health is self-explanatory, we should think holistically about health. First, think about physical health. I know we've had to have this discussion in our family because one of our teenage sons once told us he didn't need as much sleep as he once did when he was very young. However, studies say that he needs between 8 and 10 hours of sleep every night.[19] When you sleep, your brain is able to heal itself. It can heal and deal with some of the things that you were experiencing that day or overstimulation that you were experiencing. The proper amount of sleep is not just so that you're not tired; it's also so that you have better brain health.

Along with the need for downtime for our brains is the subject of obesity. We're not going to belabor this point. Still, the amount of screen time or video game playing and the overall physical health and well-being of young people are related. Today, there are so many more opportunities to be sedentary. We know there is a correlation between movement and weight. The less activity, the more likelihood there will be physical side effects. That's why games that get your kids moving are better for them if they are going to play video games. Many virtual reality games or sports-type games are geared this way and, therefore, can be positive. If you have a child like our youngest, it doesn't matter what he's playing because when he plays anything, he's jumping around, running, and bouncing into things. That's a good thing because he can get up and move. Please understand that not all video games are bad. When it comes to the topic of physical health, it's what our children are doing or not doing while they play them.

Regarding mental health, we need to discuss the amount of time spent and the correlation to happiness. It is an interesting study.

- 68% of teens say that chatting with friends can cheer them up.
- 89% of teens report that something online made them happy.
- 82% of teens report something online had made them excited. [20]

We know that what they see plays into mental health. The reality is that what you and I see plays into our mental health, too.

Young people today live with a fear that is referred to as FOMO, fear of missing out. It's rooted in seeing what their friends are doing and being afraid of what they're missing. They think, "If I'm not posting, what am I missing?" Or, "I didn't see it. Why didn't I see it?" Or, "I'm missing out. I feel like I'm always constantly missing out on something," or worse, it's the idea of, "Hey, I put a picture up, but it only has five likes. Sally put one up, and it has 50 likes. It was us at the same event. Why did Sally get more likes than I got?"

All people want affirmation; teenagers, however, especially hunger for acceptance. They view their acceptance based upon the number of likes, comments, or shares their post got. They're not the only ones that do this. In my work, social media is the number one way we advertise. I'm constantly looking at how our posts or advertisements are doing. Even doing this from a business perspective, I still pay attention to likes, comments, and shares. Depending on the numbers, I evaluate why specific posts do better. I considered what time it was posted and what it was about. I have the luxury of evaluating it, putting it down, and walking away. Can you imagine constantly living in a state of thinking, "What am I missing out on?" And then, "Why didn't I get the likes?" You can imagine how those thoughts might affect self-esteem or self-image. Can you imagine living in a world where you are waiting for others to constantly affirm you? That's what teenagers live with—stress or emotional hurt. You might think someone is not bothered. Everybody doesn't express it the same way, but they still have that challenge.

Cyberbullying is a topic that fits under the mental health category. It's a very real health issue. A lot of people have been either bullied or have bullied others.

- 77.5% of teens report that someone posted mean or hurtful comments about them.
- 70.4% of teens said someone had spread rumors about them online.
- 69.1% of teens report having been intentionally embarrassed or humiliated online by someone.
- 66.4% of teens said someone intentionally excluded them from a group text or group chat.
- 55.5% of teens said someone repeatedly contacted them via text or online after they were told to stop.[21]

Unfortunately, we have seen too many cases where people thought about or tried ending their life because of online harassment and bullying. It ought not to be, it shouldn't be, and it's up to us as parents to ensure that that's not a part of what our children do. How will they tell us about it if we're not engaged? I don't have the time to flesh this one out, but some of the stories I read would bring you to tears. In an article I read, a teenage boy was playing a video game. In that game, they encouraged you to go to another chat room. In that chat room, gamers used very obscene language and made degrading comments about everyone. Other gamers began attacking him, and he didn't know what to do. Eventually his parents (which they should have done earlier) got on because they saw something come up on a device. They found out that their teenage son had gotten involved with a world of gaming that was consuming him and surrounding him with bullying. As soon as his mother brought it up, the teenage boy melted in her arms and started crying because he didn't know how to tell them what was happening. That breaks my heart and makes me realize that what we're talking about is not just did you win or lose the game? We're talking about so much more when it comes to the arena of digital media.

Conclusion

Like Lego blocks, you and I, along with our children, were designed by God with the need to be connected to others. God knew this when He created us, and I firmly believe that's one of the greatest blessings the body of Christ offers. When we are connected to our brothers and sisters in Christ, we gain encouragement to press on toward eternity.

Connection is not the problem; however, with the technological boom since 1995, the snowball of connection has continued to grow and grow. Our homes are becoming more dependent on technology, even with some being built and marketed as "smart homes." The convenience of telling a computer to lock the door, adjust the thermostat, turn the lights on, and even turn the oven is such a draw that, as a culture, we are only going to be drawn deeper in our reliance upon technology.
As our society rapidly moves in this direction, our connectedness will continue to increase. As adults, we must be cognizant of the impact this will have on our physical and emotional health. We will need to set boundaries for ourselves, so that we are not consumed by such.

We must also be keenly aware of this for our children. Technology will become an even more significant part of their lives, and the life-changing impacts we are seeing today will only become more apparent. We must not only be aware of where we are today, but we must also empower ourselves with a purposeful plan that will teach our children to set God-honoring boundaries that are healthy and realistic. When we do so, we will help our children better navigate these digital waters, not just today, but also in the future when they are no longer living in our house.

3
Safety Must Be Prioritized

I want you to imagine your child or your grandchild walking through a known mine field. If they were walking through a mine field, first of all, you would understand the consequences that maybe they would not understand, because you've heard the stories, you've seen the pictures, perhaps maybe you even served in the military where a mine field was a real thing. However, your children don't, your grandchildren don't, because chances are they don't have those experiences or knowledge. And so what they do is they approach this field just like any other field. Does that concern you? It ought to concern all of us. If you understand that it's a mine field but your children don't, the reality is ignorance is not always bliss. Sometimes ignorance can literally get you killed or can cause a lot of damage. And that's where someone who knows more has got to be willing to stand up and say something. "Hey, that is a mine field! Do not go play there!" And if you had to cross the field, you would tell your child, "Walk where I walk" because you hope that your experiences in life allow you to detect and discern where the danger is.

We live in a day and age of a mine field. But it's a digital mine field. And that doesn't mean that there's not good, nor do I want to overinflate the dangers or scare you, but I want to be very clear about what we're dealing with. We're not dealing with an innocent playground. We're not dealing with this idea of a community park or an amusement park where everybody is happy to be off of work and just want to have a good time. Sometimes it's a situation where people are not interested in your good time; they're only interested in their good time. And sometimes individuals fall into pits, they fall into snares, they get entangled, or they step on a land mine.

The reality is I want to avoid as much of that as possible within my home, and I know you do within yours. With this lesson I want to heighten your senses. I want you to be aware of what's out there and what could happen. And the first thing I want you to understand is not everybody is out there for the benefit of your child or your own personal benefit.

The Dangers Lurking

1) Child Predators

In the age of the digital world, we have dangers that lurk all around; and some of those dangers have serious, serious consequences. This particular slide that I show you here is an article that I found when I was researching internet usage, believe it or not. And it talks about how with the Corona virus individuals were thrown online with their work, their schooling, and the internet became a more integral part of our lives as fewer and fewer people got out and about. The numbers indicate that more and more people are using the internet. We should not be surprised then that the more activity on the internet, then the more likelihood of there being issues that can occur. The particular article I read was an article about child predators.

Now, you and I have heard about child predators. Chances are you've even possibly seen an ABC special or some kind of special on TV where the FBI sets up a sting posing as an underage girl and schedule a meeting. The man would show up to the meeting, maybe meet a "girl" actress, then the FBI would confirm that he came with the intent to meet an underage girl to commit sexual acts and arrest him.

Chances are you and I have heard of individuals who have been arrested for solicitation. The reality is this, people online aren't always who they say they are. Those who are in law enforcement can pretend to be someone different to catch people who are trying to do bad things. However, those who prey on children can do the same to lure young people into this false sense of security and let down their guards. Well, this danger is very, very serious.

For the first nine months of 2019, there were 15,220 cases that were reported in online enticement of children. Now, this is a small study, so I'm only giving you a sample. By 2020, this same particular study group had conducted the same study again and noticed the same trends, only this time in 2020 for just the first nine months it was at 30,236. It had doubled in one year. Why would that be the case? Well, because more and more people are online and more opportunities are being created in various apps or gaming chat sites or other chat sites. And it's not always in what you would think are the obvious sites. Sometimes child predators can lure children away through games that you and I think are quite innocent.

For instance, let's consider Minecraft. It's one of the most popular games with young people— they enjoy building these alter-reality worlds, and then they have the opportunity to explore them as they become their character. Minecraft took advantage of technology where you could actually take your phone, create a world, and then "bring it to life" by shining it in a place. I physically could walk through my Minecraft world while it was projecting in a room. I'll tell you we let our children play Minecraft. But Minecraft has been used by child predators who pretend to befriend young people and get them to let their security senses down. Here's what we did on Minecraft. My children are not allowed in the chats at all. We shut down all chats. If I ever find out there is a chat, then they know that there are going to be consequences to pay for doing what Dad said not to do. I've made a no-chat policy on purpose because I know what exists and what's potentially out there.

The idea, though, is the games are portals to reach your child. What you may not know is that when it comes to child predators, the average median age for individuals who get caught up in this is the age of 15. Now, that's a median age, which means there are some who get caught up much earlier than that and some who get caught up much later than that, even in their late teens. But either way, 15 seemed to be the average among them. This type of victimization actually occurs across every platform: social media, messaging apps, gaming platforms, and others like that. [1]

Consider the most common tactics used to entice children:

- Engaging in sexual conversation/role playing as a grooming method, rather than a goal.
- Asking children for sexually explicit images of themselves or mutually sharing images.
- Developing a rapport through compliments, discussing shared interests or "liking" their online posts, also known as grooming.
- Sending or offering sexually explicit images of themselves.
- Pretending to be younger.
- Offering an incentive such as a gift card, alcohol, drugs, lodging, transportation, or food.[2]

So children, most are young ladies, get wrapped up in trusting someone that they only know online. You'll remember in the last chapter we talked about the three areas that we need to be aware of: the brain development, the relationships, and the health. In the relationship portion, I told you that some friendships are made online only without ever meeting the person that they have befriended online. Some may be tempted to think to themselves, "Oh, they're friends online much like I'm friends with people on Facebook." No. It's not the same. With friends on Facebook, you look at their pictures, posts, likes, and interests. When your child says, "I have a friend on this game" or "We're friends through _____ (an app)", it's not to look at pictures every now and again. That's not a child predator's concept. A child predator wants to befriend them over a period of time and prep them to get them to a point where they are trapped. The predator says—do what I say or there will be major consequences. Here is an example of that.

This is an actual court case and an actual thread between a child and predator. A child predator finally revealed himself to a teenage girl and this is what he said.

> You've been tricked.
> I'm a guy, and I will e-mail all the pics you sent me to your school.
> I would not block me or delete Kik.
> Because if you do that, I'm still sending it to your school.
>
> If you obey me and do everything I want, then I will delete your pics and I will not e-mail your school. But I warn you, if you disobey me once, I will send your pics.

You'll notice the tactics of the child predator. It wasn't the concept of "Let's meet in a chat room." Child predators want underaged children to send compromising pictures or videos to them repeatedly, and if the children don't, then there is a threat. In this particular case, he threatened to send all of her pictures to her school. This teenage girl was so scared she said "Okay, what do I have to do?"

We can Monday morning quarterback all day long, right?

I know you're thinking: Why was she allowed to get involved in the first place? Where were her parents? Why were they disconnected? Why did they not know that she was doing this? That's one. The other one is this: Why did she think it was okay? Did she not know the dangers that exist today in the world? Where did she ever get that that was okay to become such friends that obviously she sent pictures that she doesn't want shared with people? I want you to understand: Child predators, those who lurk online pretending to be teenage boys and teenage girls, they will spend however long it takes to work their way into a child's life to gain their trust so that their defenses come down. From then on, it's just seen as the flirtatious, funny, safe because it's online kind of relationship so the child feels safe.

This happens more than we would like to admit, more than we would ever think it did. Remember it doesn't begin with an explicit request. If it were that obvious, then every parent would say that's not good. The problem is parents who are disconnected from what's going on in their child's online life are oftentimes surprised that their children end up in situations like this. Your children or others you know may have made some bad decisions. Remember again the prefrontal cortex and the idea of the impulse and some of the restrictions. Why do teenagers think like teenagers? It's because they're teenagers. But the idea that some adults are more than willing to take advantage of those teenagers ought to scare us, right?

Bottom line: You need to be engaged with your children and grandchildren on social media. You need to have their information. You need to have log-in information, passwords, be friends with them, but you also need to be aware that it is possible for people to create fake accounts and only let you see what they want yet live a different way in another account. You say how do I know if that's going on? And ultimately at the end of the day, it's because you have a relationship with your child offline, too.

Keep in mind, even good kids can make bad decisions. We need to remember this. If your child or your grandchild has made that decision, gotten wrapped up in this, I want to emphasize something to you: No matter what decisions they made, this should never be pegged on that teenage child. Because there was someone who was setting a trap for her, preying on him, and the reality is they fell prey. Ultimately at the end of the day, they should have been aware and known the dangers, but it's the predator's fault that the predator is a predator. We need to be able to look our children in the eyes if they ever get caught in that and say that we still love them and that we're here for them and that we're going to get them help.

2) Posting About Your Children Online

The second mine in the mine field that I want to bring to the surface is what is posted about our children online that can actually lead to information harvesting and to child predators having an easier time in working their way into your child's life. Let's consider an example. You want to know more about a person that you met (also known as stalking, even among adults!). If you look at social media posts that person has made, you'll learn key information such as first and last names. Through the pictures, you'll be able to see who that person is and what that person looks like. Often, you'll be able to find out where that person lives—if it's not a direct address, it will at least be the city and state. From there, just with a little bit more work, you could find out what his actual address is. You'll not only learn about the person you met and stalked, but you'll also learn who they're married to and who their relatives are. You'll learn interests—What are his hobbies? What does he like to listen to? Has he followed any shows? You can also learn about his work, because sometimes we'll post that on social media.

Beyond that, though, you'll learn about his children. You'll learn the children's names because parents love to post about the accomplishments of their children. Since we already know the exact address of the home, we can easily find the schools close to the address. If his children aren't home-schooled, with some minimal research you could probably locate the exact school his children attend, the grades they are in, and possibly who their teachers are. We would most likely be able to discern the ages of the children because of the social media posts made regarding birthday celebrations. I can most likely find out the interest of the children and pinpoint their after-school activities. The reality is, with just a small amount of time spent on a social media page of a person, we could discover so much about their family.

Here's what's sad. Most of that information is posted online before your children ever have a choice as to whether they want to have a social media footprint, because you started posting when they were babies. You gave names; you gave birthdays. If a person were a child predator and they wanted to harvest information about your family, it would not be very difficult at all. The sad part is that many parents and grandparents aren't even thinking of the potential dangers when we use social media for ourselves. We want our children to be guarded. We install filters to help and set time limits; however, we are often the most guilty about opening the door to online dangers for our children because of what we freely offer.

How scary would it be if somebody e-mailed you a picture of your own child and said, "I know where he goes to school and I know how he gets home?" What would go through your mind? What you share about your children and your grandchildren, if you're not locked down and secure, is public access to whoever wants to find it. And all of that happens most of the time before your children are even old enough to decide for themselves. Now, does that mean you should never post pictures of your children online? No, I don't think it necessarily means that. But this is what it does mean: You must go into your social media accounts, locate the privacy settings on those accounts, and set those to protect the information that you put out.

I think you need to be cautious. You be responsible about what you post. Do you have to post everything your child does? No, you don't. But Joe, you say, what if so-and-so thinks I'm not proud? Well, let so-and-so think what they're going to think, okay? The reality is your job is to protect your children. Let's call this lesson Safety Must Be Prioritized—even above what other people think of you. Because once this information is out, it's out.

3) Pornography

Obviously, pornography is so prevalent in our society when roughly 28,258 users are watching pornography every second, and there is $3,075.64 spent on pornography every second on the internet. Because roughly 40 million Americans regularly visit these kind of sites, and 35% of all internet downloads related to pornography, the third mine in the mine field of the online world must be addressed.[3]

It's no surprise that adults have become ensnared in this trap of Satan. The following percentage of men say they view pornography at least once a month:
- 79% of 18- to 30-year-olds
- 67% of 31- to 49-year-olds
- 49% of 50- to 68-year-olds [4]

The statistics pertaining to women are interesting, though. The following percentage of women say they view pornography at least once a month:
- 76% of 18- to 30-year-olds
- 16% of 31- to 49-year-olds
- 4% of 50- to 68-year-olds.[5]

But you say, "I thought this was just a man's problem." I've been following these numbers since about 2008 or 2009, trying to keep up with statistics and areas of growth in the pornographic industry. In the early days, the numbers did show that pornography was predominantly a male problem. But then the pornographic industry started to pursue new clientele. They sought other ways to expand their businesses, and so more women went into ownerships of pornographic companies. They did so because they believed they could produce pornography that would attract a female audience.

With this focused effort, I'm seeing a much, much greater percentage of younger women who are also caught in Satan's trap. This change is partly because younger generations are viewing pornography in a more favorable light than it has ever been viewed from a moral perspective. In other words, they think it really isn't a bad thing. There are other things in this world that are worse than pornography is their thought. This is a big deal even within the church.

This became very apparent to me one year when I was speaking at a North Carolina camp, and some teenage boys came up and confessed to have been struggling with pornography. There were probably six or seven of them all saying the same thing. What was sad is they were talking about it as if it was no big deal. And when asked where they first heard about it—where did they share information—they said people at school. That's how prevalent this is. They can talk about football, about the newest show streaming, about the new thing that's going on in the school with this teacher or that teacher, and oh, by the way, they throw in a conversation about another free pornographic site.

By now, the fact that teens view or have viewed pornographic material is not as big a shock to many adults; however, most adults don't think their child falls into the statistics. Please don't think I am insinuating that all your children have walked into this jungle of deception. I am most definitely not, but I would encourage you to be informed and aware of the vastness of the trap that is out there.

Consider the following statistics revealing the percentage of young people who have viewed pornography:

- 50% of 11- to 13-year-olds
- 65% of 14- to 15-year-olds
- 78% of 16- to 17-year-olds [6]

For whatever reason, parents are disillusioned about these percentages. They're disconnected in understanding that it is very prevalent; and therefore it's very easy for their teenagers to get trapped. Please recognize—your young people don't have to go searching for pornography to find pornography. If your child just does a regular Google search and types in something, the video sites, image or video search engines will show images that you'll never see in their history, but they can look at them. If they click on it, then you'll see it. You might see the search if you pay attention to that; but most kids know how to erase their history portion of their computer or their phones. And so even through Google porn can be accessed. These images, though, can even be sent through video game chat sites. You need to be aware of that. It's not just that they went looking for it.

We must address the disconnect between parents' perceptions of their children's pornographic viewing and the actual viewing. This is what blew my mind. 75 percent of parents felt their child would have not seen pornography online. 75. Three out of four parents. Here's what the children of those parents said, though. 53 percent said they had in fact seen pornography. So three out of the four parents are saying. "My child's never seen it," and one out of every two kids have said, "Yes, I have." Why do parents not know? And before we start beating ourselves up, the reality is it happens before you know it. Most first-time exposure to pornography is not because they went looking for pornography. Instead, they happened upon something that was interesting and odd, and it drew them into the pornography world where they now want to know more and they want to see more. It's scary, the land mine of pornography.

4) Apps

The last category to consider are the apps that your children and your grandchildren download on phones and on tablets. There are plenty of these sites out there that will tell you the worst ones to be aware of. As you consider these specific ones, remember that many of the gaming apps your children and grandchildren download and install on their devices have a chat component to them which allows other people, some you may know and others you may not know, to interact with your child. I highly advise either turning this setting off and having a conversation with your young person regarding the dangers of accepting messages and chatting with people they and your family do not personally know.

Whisper is an app you may have seen on your children's phones. I encourage you—don't look at just the icon, because icons change, and they update. Whisper was created for 17 and up, and its motto is: "Share secrets, express yourself, meet new people." Why should you be worried about that? It allows for creative expression, which is good; but it can also take overly personal content and make it viral. The app also shows a user's location. Whisper lets a user set up an anonymous account to make their messages or confessions overlap an image or a graphic. Then other people can like it or not like it. It reveals information to the world about them.

Another one needing considered is Kik, an instant messaging app. It's wildly popular amongst teenagers today. Whether or not your teens have it or not, you need to be aware that it exists. And they like it because it's cross-platform. In other words, it's not just an iPhone only and you can only communicate with people if they have an iPhone or an IOS device, but it also works with those who have androids or Windows. It's cross-platform, so young people seem to like that. You don't even need a cell phone service to use it.

So if you're kind of the way we have been in our family, the first thing our children have gotten were iPod Touches, they were not iPhones; and we may not even do that anymore. But the idea is that you can engage in this particular app without it having cell phone service. So don't think because you only gave your kids a tablet that you saved them. The reality is you did not. They can still get on the internet, they can still talk, they can still message outside of needing that cell phone service.

Why should you be worried about Kik?

A user of this can create an account name that's not associated with a phone number, making authenticating a user's identity difficult. You remember our child predator portion of this lesson? The anonymous nature of the app has made it easy for sexual predators to contact children and teens or for the children to be threatened and cyber bullied. While it's very popular, it's also very dangerous.

The last two I'll draw your attention to are Grindr and Tinder. These are apps that were basically designed for what young people today call "hookups" or casual sexual encounters. In these apps a user can create a profile, connect with people, and decide whether or not they want to meet up. So why would these even be an issue with teenagers? Because teenagers love to gravitate towards older things, to think they're more grown up than they are, and to reach for what they believe is more mature. The same is true in apps—they want to "be mature."

Grindr and Tender are very similar apps. They're flirting apps used to meet people through GPS location service. Grindr has the same exact security issues as Tinder (remember these apps are strictly for adults), so these apps with GPS location make it easy for an adult to contact someone else who's on the app. There are others we could look at. Most are not totally evil, but they all have dangers for our children. Whether it be through a message component or through content, we as parents must be protective and proactive for our children. If we're not aware, then we will never be able to guard our child through a mine field. From that standpoint, safety has to be prioritized, because if it's not, then there's going to be problems.

Tools to Help Keep Your Family Safe

What can we do? We could kick the internet out of our houses, but very few people are even going to consider that option. Therefore if we're going to operate in this world of the internet with cell phones, with tablets, with home internet, we better do something to make it safer for our families. What can we do? I'm going to give you four things that you can do right now to help; these are workable, helpful tools for us to prioritize safety.

1) DNS Resolver

A DNS (Domain Name System) resolver is a more advanced option; however, with a little effort, this could be a very viable and effective tool for your situation. One DNS resolver I would recommend is called 1.1.1.1, and, yes, that is its name. You have to get a little techie on your own with this one, because you actually will change something on your internet router. And I know I've just scared some of you pretty badly just saying those words. Here's the way this one works. You have what is called a DNS (Domain Name System) on your router. Every router has one. It's kind of like the phone book for the internet. You can actually go in and change the numbers on the DNS. And when you change the numbers, it will impact what that will allow through your router.

It might help you to know that the internet doesn't operate and communicate like you and I communicate. In other words, you and I talk with words. The internet talks with numbers and codes. And so it will translate a word. You and I have a word; it has a number that goes along with that word. Here's the number for Google (8.8.8.8 or 8.8.4.4). Every time the router sees that number, it will translate that as Google. So if you want to take care of your family, then you've got to talk numbers and not words.

So, in order to use the DNS to help guard your family, you go into your router and change your DNS to 1.1.1.1, and what that will do is through the app that this company has, it will allow you to block adult sites through your router, and it will take care of malware (intrusive software that is designed to damage your computer), which a lot of different web sites have and want to place that on what you're doing for information harvesting. 1.1.1.1 is free. It may be a little intimidating, but you can usually figure out how to log into your router.

2) Home Monitor Devices

Another helpful resource that I highly recommend to you is the Circle Home Plus. It's come a long way—they have a second generation now, and they have the plus edition. You plug this device into your router through one of the ports in the back of your router, and then you download their app. When you download the app, it detects every device connected to your internet. So for example your son's gaming system, your daughter's cell phone, your cell phone, the TV in the main room, the TV in the bonus room, the TV in the master bedroom, all computers and tablets —all will be in listed in the app. Then you can go through and set limits on any device that is connected to your internet in your home.

One of the great aspects of the Circle Home Plus is that it also works with mobile devices. If you can control the Internet in your home, that's great. However, if your son has a cell phone with cell service and a data plan, then all he's got to do is turn off home wi-fi and start operating off cellular service, he can look at anything, and it's not blocked. The difference maker with the Circle Home Plus is it also takes care of mobile devices anywhere. It's a little more expensive, but you can buy it several ways. You can pay per month, pay per year, or you can buy a lifetime access to this.

Here's what we liked about it. I could set time limits on the Internet. So let's say you don't want your son or daughter to have a device in their room after you go to bed. Otherwise, when you go to sleep, they're going to be on their phone very late and not sleep, or maybe that's when they're getting on the internet, potentially doing things they shouldn't be doing. Here's what's great about it. Let's say I want to lock down my son's phone, his game system, and the TV. I could literally set it where all the Internet is shut off to those devices at a certain time, and it doesn't turn back on until the time I set in the morning.

3) Monitoring Apps

Family monitoring apps such as Bark or Family Orbit give you the ability to monitor all your child's phone activities. You can view calls, websites, and text history, allowing you to keep an eye on the sort of content that your child has been viewing. Along with these features, a family monitoring app can allow you to use the real-time map feature so that you know where your children are or at least where their device is located.

One specific monitoring app I'll mention to you is Covenant Eyes. We use this on all our devices—mobile devices, tablets, and computers. It was designed as an accountability program. However, what I love about it is it operates on what's called a VPN (Virtual Private Network), which serves to encrypt your internet traffic and mask your identity to those who may wish to harvest your information. For people who harvest information, the VPN helps defeat their efforts. Certain internet search engines also do this, such as Duck Duck Go. That also operates in a similar fashion: it cuts down on tracking. Google tracks everything, just so you know. You want to know why it is that all of a sudden you were talking about dogs, and on your social media page articles and ads about dogs came up? If you think that they're not listening to you, you're wrong. What you search for, they see. The goal is to secure as much of that interaction as possible. Covenant Eyes is a monitoring app that operates on a VPN, which allows for its filtering or its accountability to occur.

So here's the way Covenant Eyes works. I can go in behind the scenes and set limitations on content that will be allowed to come in under that log-in device. And as long as they search with Covenant Eyes as their internet browser (the ones that come installed on your phone/tablets can be hidden behind a password), their internet searches are protected. With the VPN, Covenant Eyes also monitors activity through other apps. The shortfall is if the material that comes through an app is not what you want your children to see, but it is not the level that the Covenant Eyes will block, then your kids will still be able to see it. For instance, if on Covenant Eyes I blocked pornography, then it is still possible for pictures of people in their underwear to come through because it would not necessarily be lumped into the internet's definition of pornography. So there may be some instances that it wouldn't block.

Here's what I do like about it, though, is that I get a report once a month on the activity that my children participate in, and Erin and

I get a report on each other about what happens with our internet activity. Also Covenant Eyes takes screen shots. So it's not just on the internet search, but they're taking screen shots randomly, and they will send those along with the report, to which you can then see what phone looked at it, what was it that they looked at, and when was it accessed.

Now, nothing is perfect, but I will tell you this: It at least allows for some good conversation. You remember I told you the goal is to win the hearts of your children? I want my children to make good decisions when I'm not there, right? I also want to take out as many opportunities to fail as possible; but I ultimately want them to make good decisions when I'm not there, because my goal is to raise them to make good decisions when they go off to college, or when they get married. What I want to do is I want them to know that Dad can see. Now, does that mean Dad can see everything? No. Nothing is foolproof in that sense. But I want them to know Dad can find out. Dad can look at histories. Dad can look at the report that comes through Covenant Eyes. And I tell them, if you ever get blocked from something, you're always going to do better to come tell me first than to let me find out about it in my report. And the whole reason I do that is because I want them to know sometimes they could get blocked for something that they didn't mean to and I'm not going to overreact. Because if I overreact, guess who they're not coming to anymore? They're not coming to me.

I also want them to know I get it and I appreciate their telling me. And then I also want them to understand that I can see, because I want them to think, "If I want to look at that, Dad might be able to see that." But I don't want them to make the right decisions just because I can see it. I want them ultimately to make the right decisions because they want to be pleasing to God. And I want to translate that to God knows and God sees, even if I don't.

4) Parental Settings on the Device:

I always encourage families to explore the parental settings that come already installed on the device. For those who use Apple products, the Content & Privacy Restrictions in Screen Time allow you to block or limit specific apps and features on your child's device. Along with this feature, you can also restrict the settings on your iPhone, iPad, or iPod touch for explicit content, purchases and downloads, and privacy. Family Sharing is another great setting that allows for all purchases made through the iOS App Store to have to be approved by the owner of the account—that would be you the parent.

Those using Android devices, you can limit data usage under the Network & Internet option under Settings. Once you're in the Network & Internet menu, select Data Usage and then Mobile Data Usage. From there, tap the cog wheel in the upper right corner and select the data limit you desire for the device. Once the data limit is reached, the apps and games that require more data usage then you've allowed will not be able to work. This feature is seen as a "time-limiting" concept.

Other parent control features can be found by selecting Settings, Users and Accounts, and creating a new user by clicking Add User. Once here, you can select the option to create a Restricted User Account and select what apps and games you would like to be shown or hidden on the device. All of this is protected by a PIN you select, so make sure you do not select a PIN your child might guess if they get curious.

In the Google Play store, you will find the Parental Settings by clicking on the three horizontal lines in the top left after opening the Google Play store app. Once here, you will need to select Settings and then Parental Controls. You will enter a PIN once again to make sure your selections are kept and only changed by someone who knows your PIN.

Along with the parental controls that come built into the device, many of your cell carriers will also offer family settings that may be of benefit.

There are options. Which one would I recommend to you? All of them. I don't believe in one defense when it comes to the dangers that we are up against. But none of these can replace parental involvement. Not a single one of those can replace your knowing what's going on in your child's devices, you knowing what's going on in their gaming. You might not even like gaming or other things your child is involved in. I don't care. Do you love your children? And if your children are going to be into gaming, you need to be informed about what's going on in that device.

The idea is this: The goal is their heart. The goal is that God will say, "I'm not ashamed to be called their God." The goal is to inherit the incorruptible, the crown of righteousness. The goal is to glorify God. The goal is to get all your family to Heaven. And so you'll do whatever it takes. The internet's not going away. I've been asked if I believe we'll ever return to a time where the internet was not such an integral part of our environment? The answer is no. That's not going to happen. It's going to become much more an integral part of our world. So you and I must take the steps to protect and defend our families.

Be Aware: Anxiety, Addiction & Reputation

Imagine, if you will, a sponge—a seemingly ordinary household item with a surprisingly profound metaphorical significance. As mundane as it may seem, the sponge exemplifies how our children, like sponges, absorb the influences around them. This simple object—whether it's used to wash dishes, clean cars, or scrub tubs—shares one crucial characteristic: It absorbs its environment. When placed in water, a sponge will inevitably soak up the liquid, and even when wrung out, traces of the liquid remain in it.

Now, with that in mind, I want to explore three critical aspects of our children's interaction with their digital environment: anxiety, addiction, and reputation. In the age of the digital world and the technological advances which we are in, these three concepts are crucial to the mental and physical well-being of the individuals within our homes. I'll even go so far as to say those three ideas are crucial to what happens next for your children as they continue growing through puberty, with the plethora of hormones rushing through their brains.

In the previous chapter, we investigated the concept of digital footprints. You'll recall the warning concerning individuals who want to harvest information and possibly bring harm to our children. They can go online and get whatever you and I post, including information about our children: schools, ages, birthdays, sports teams, and much more. Well…the topic of digital footprints needs to be a part of this discussion as well because not only are the footprints used by individuals who want to harvest information for their purposes; they can also be harvested by peers at your children's school. This is significant because a peer can take a picture you posted of your child that is embarrassing and circulate it around the school. Just like with most things in the digital world, an embarrassing picture is easy to share and attracts the attention of other young people at their school. Before too long, the image will be used by other children to try and publicly humiliate your child.

Technology today creates situations like these, and we must discuss the effects in the lives of many young people. No parent wants their child to go through bullying as described above. In like manner, no parent wants their child to experience an increase amount of anxiety, become addicted, or even suffer a ruined reputation. However, because our children are like sponges soaking up their environment, we must be aware of the impact being so connected is having on them.

Be Aware: Anxiety and Its Growing Effect

Merriam Webster's Online Dictionary defines *anxiety* as "an abnormal and overwhelming sense of apprehension and fear often marked by physical signs (such as tension, sweating, and increased pulse rate), by doubt concerning the reality and nature of the threat, and by self-doubt about one's capacity to cope with it." In other words, anxiety is an unhealthy fear about what may or may not be a threat. While fear is experienced by all of us, it becomes unhealthy when you become immobilized and hopeless in dealing with that fear. It's unhealthy when the tension, the sweating, the heart rate, the lack of self-worth, or the feeling that you are not capable of overcoming it consumes you. Repeatedly, the reports are showing that the more you and your children are connected to technology, the more you experience this tension, fear, and apprehension.

The statistics are quite interesting:
- 61% of teenagers already feel a lot of pressure to get good grades.
- 29% feel a lot of pressure to look good.
- 28% feel pressure to fit in socially.
- 2% are already bearing the weight of pressure to be involved in extracurricular activities and to be good at sports.[2]

Now, none of those have anything to do with a digital footprint or the digital age; just know that during the teen years, our children are already under so many pressures that breed anxiety or fears. Part of that is because young people in their teen years don't feel comfortable. They have internal questions. "What will this person think?" "What is that group saying about me?" "Why didn't they invite me to this outing?" "Why is it that no boys like me?" "Why is it that no girls like me?" "Oh that guy, he's the good looking one?" Thoughts like these consume them and cause them to think negatively about themselves with all the hormonal and developmental changes they experience.

As much as I would love to tell you that I could give you a Scripture or statistics that would get rid of the need that teenagers feel to compare themselves to other people, I can't. That's in part because the developmental stage known as adolescence is weird. They know they aren't supposed to judge themselves by others. But when Dr. Evil Pituitary Gland kicks in, life seems to become very unbalanced. As your child's attention gradually begins to turn away from focusing on family relationships to paying more and more attention to peer relationships, this awkwardness is only amplified. Add to this the fact our children are growing up in a super connected society thanks to the digital age, you have a perfect storm for anxiety and depression to creep in and take root.

Therefore the topic of anxiety has been the subject of much study conducted by child counselors and psychologists. The question usually centers around what comes first—the chicken or the egg. In other words, did digital media cause young people to be anxious, or were people already anxious and digital media only compounded the severity and pressures?

Either way, as parents we've got to have this discussion, because when it comes to social media:
- 45% of teens feel overwhelmed by the drama on social media.
- 26% say social media makes them feel worse about their own lives.
- 43% feel pressure to post content that makes them look good.
- 37% feel pressure to share things that will get likes and comments.[3]

If you think for one minute that young people aren't concerned about whether anyone liked or commented on their post, then you're missing a major concept: in the life of an adolescent, there is a strong desire to be accepted. Consider what that does to their mental and emotional well-being. They don't want to be left out. As a matter of fact, studies have shown that the three biggest fears of adolescents are: being made fun of, being left out, and being made to feel like they're not good enough. In other words, they don't want to be excluded. Instead, they want to be accepted and included.

Teenagers always talk about their individuality but consider this weird phenomenon. Have you ever noticed that those wanting to express their individuality often flock to other people who look the same, sound the same, watch the same TV shows, listen to the same music, and play the same video games? It's like—"I want to be individual, but I only identify with everybody who plays Minecraft.

Individuality is great, and it's a need; but ultimately at the end of the day, teenagers don't want to be on an island. Even individuals who say they want to be on an island may color their hair, dress in black, paint their fingernails, and they hang out with other people who do the exact same thing. That's because there's a need to be accepted in adolescence. That need doesn't change just because we become adults. We want to be accepted just as do our children.

> *"I pretty much just post stuff that makes me look good and makes me look my ideal self."*[4] -16-year-old boy

What is this young man referring to when he says "my ideal self?"

Interestingly enough, the distorted view of life made normalized by social media has entrapped many young people. Their desire to be perceived a certain way causes a great deal of social anxiety. With "Likes" and "Shares" being used as a barometer to judge their acceptance by their peers, the drive to present oneself in a certain light is causing them to go to tremendous measures to stage pictures or use filters to alter reality. While photographers have been using photo editing techniques to highlight, change lighting, and offer shading to enhance their digital pictures for some time, the use of them by teens is growing in magnitude. There is a direct correlation between the anxiety a teen feels and their filtered presentation of themselves.

Along with this strong desire to be accepted is the desire to be included. As we said earlier, teenagers do not like to be left out. When their friends go out to eat, they want to be included. When there's a group of teens going to a movie, it affirms them as being accepted when they are invited to come along. However, just as it is affirming to be included, it is detrimental to be left out, causing serious emotional hurt and pain, which is another contributing factor to the increased levels of anxiety among young people today.

With social media, texting, and messaging apps being ingrained in our daily lives, teenagers are ever attentive to who's liking or sharing images. They are also very tuned into who's in the pictures, especially if it is a group by whom they themselves want to be accepted. Psychologists have identified this reality by the acronym FoMO or Fear of Missing Out, according to the *World Journal of Clinical Cases*:

> The concept of FoMO explores the fear of social exclusion. Through social media, there is continuous awareness of what an individual may be missing in terms of a good time which researcher phrases as 'it creates distorted perceptions of edited lives of others.'
>
> The 'round the clock' nature of these communication may lead to feeling lonely and inadequate through highlighting others activities and popularity and comparison of oneself to others, leading to vicious cycle of compulsive checking and engagement.[5]

Unfortunately, the more time a young person spends online trying to post just the right picture and like or share just the right picture of their friends, the more likely they are to suffer with FoMO. It's sad that the very place they go to be connected causes them more and more emotional strain such as anxiety.

If your child/teen is demonstrating signs of suffering with abnormal levels of anxiety, you most likely need to be aware that their online habits could be a major contributor to their pain. But how do you know if they are suffering with an unhealthy level of anxiety? Consider the following as you reflect on yourself and your child.

Signs of anxiety in teens include these four major key areas:

Emotional signs

These include signs such as the individual not getting excited often, being unhappy, may seem depressed, seem agitated, anxious, aloof, or irritable. Individuals who exhibit emotional signs of anxiety get angry and overwhelmed easily by simple things and may also feel helpless and hopeless about the situation.

Physical signs

The physical signs of anxiety include tiredness, fatigue, headaches, constipation, nausea, dizziness, palpitations, or loss of appetite. Your teen may lose interest in sports and other physical activities as well. Some teens may lose or gain weight, while girls may experience a change in their menstrual cycle.

Behavioral changes

Behavioral changes may include fidgeting, nervous habits like nail biting, restless pacing, moving around constantly, or others. Crying, isolating self from friends and family, being moody or easily irritable, not bothered about their appearance, and not showing as much interest in activities that give them pleasure could also indicate stress and anxiety.

Cognitive symptoms

Stress in teens can also impact their cognitive abilities such as memory. If you think that they are neglecting their chores or being careless, consider if they may be stressed. It may not be they're trying to be disobedient; it may be because something else is going on in their life. Other cognitive symptoms may include being irrational, having an inability to focus, having a negative perspective, and exhibiting poor judgement.[6]

Trends show that a decrease in happiness is occurring in America among adolescents, to the extent that some individuals say that we are on the brink of a major mental crisis with young people. Am I telling you that every young person is sad? No. What I'm trying to tell you is this: The studies are showing that the onset of the digital age did not make it easier. That means as parents, we've got to be that much more involved and in tune with the emotional well-being of our children.

Be Aware: Addiction & the Signs That Show It

Another subject people who study this do not necessarily agree on—what comes first, the chicken or the egg. Are individuals who have addictive tendencies already expressing those, and digital media is another area the addiction is exhibited, or has the digital media sucked them in, causing an addiction? In other words, do they have addictive tendencies, and are they an obsessive person? Were they already expressing addictive tendencies before they used digital media, or did digital media cause the addiction?

The study of addictions and their impact on the human brain is such an interesting study. We can become addicted to anything. Do you know you can be addicted to shopping? You can be addicted to shoes. Did you know you can be addicted to hobbies like fishing? You can be addicted to fast food. When you leave for work that day, it's almost like your car finds its way to a fast-food restaurant, right? Maybe you find yourself eating out quite a bit during the day, and your job requires that, so you've fed your body the sugars and the fats, and your body has adjusted to that taste. You can become addicted to anything.

The reason is your brain releases a chemical called dopamine. Dopamine is one of the "reward chemicals" your brain releases that makes you feel great. You have the receptors in your brain that receive that because you've wired those receptacles a certain way. Think of it this way: If you have ever seen water flowing across the ground, you know that water will travel the pathway of least resistance. As water goes over the ground, it will eventually erode out a ditch where it has continually been flowing. If you want to change that and change the terrain, you've got to change the direction of the flow of the water. Otherwise, the water will always want to go in the ditch created.

It is same with an addiction. You have conditioned your brain to release dopamine upon certain behaviors. Your brain has been receiving dopamine in that fashion with that behavior for long enough that when that occurs, you feel, "Oh, this is great." And when it doesn't happen, you hunger for that dopamine. The way an addiction cycle works is this: The one who's addicted wants the high, so they do what they have to to get the high. That solves their problem briefly until the high is gone; their body craves the high again, and they do the behavior again to get it. For instance, a person addicted to video games might feel a rush of excitement and pleasure when they start playing, and when they stop, they might feel restless or irritable, craving that same rush again. Do you know that science has even found that you and I can be addicted to things like video games? I didn't say you just like playing them. You can be addicted to them, where your brain literally has that ditch carved out, and the dopamine is released upon that stimuli.

Interestingly, when we start talking about the digital age, addiction is a part of that discussion. Now, over 90% of children and teenagers in the United States today play video games, and they spend a substantial amount of time playing them.[7] And if you're curious about my house, do I allow video games? The answer is yes. Here's why. Everything I just told you is still being debated in psychological journals; one study will say one thing, and another study will say something else. These debates often revolve around the nature of addiction, whether it's a result of pre-existing tendencies or a consequence of exposure to digital media. There's not enough evidence to come to a hard and fast conclusion that this is what is going on.

Verizon, a huge telecommunications provider, reported that during COVID-19 there was a 75% increase in online gaming activity.[8] We've already addressed the impact of COVID-19 on the digital age regarding how much time our children now spend with technology. I firmly believe we will never see pre-pandemic levels again in America. Part of that is because people adjusted during the pandemic. People adjusted, and they called the new levels the "new normal."

As a matter of fact, there's a phrase for this called "Internet Gaming Disorder," where playing immersive games is done to an unhealthy degree. This disorder is characterized by a lack of control over gaming, prioritizing gaming over other activities, and continuing to game despite negative consequences. While there have been some discussions among psychological journals as to whether or not this should be a diagnosable disorder, it has yet to be decided. In 2013, the journal that psychologists use to diagnose and explain the world of psychology said that Internet Gaming Disorder was worthy of further study. In other words, it made their honorable mention list, but it didn't make their list as a disorder. However, the World Health Organization has included Internet Gaming Disorder in its most recent international classification of diseases.

The World Health Organization says that in order to classify excessive gaming as a disorder or disease, they have some criteria. One, it gets in the way of other activities. Does your gaming get in the way of other activities? Another criteria is the gaming continues despite negative consequences, such as impairment in personal, family, social, educational, occupational, or other vital areas of life. To be a disorder, it has to be evident for at least 12 months. So if you say, "My child is consumed," that should be a red flag. It's not—"My child likes to play video games." It's the idea: How does your child respond when you tell them to get off the internet? How do they react?

How do you know if you're addicted? Let's consider some questions.

- Do you have a preoccupation with gaming? Is that what you think about? When your child gets home from school, what's the first thing they want to do immediately? When they wake up in the morning, what's the first thing they want to do? What's the first thing they want to do in their free time? Is there a preoccupation with gaming?
- Are there withdrawal symptoms when gaming is taken away or not possible? Do you notice sadness, anxiety, and irritability? I know we're talking about teens, but have you ever seen a young child who was so used to playing games on a parent's phone or a grandparent's iPad that when told no that child threw a fit?
- Is there increasing tolerance—the need to spend more time gaming to satisfy the urge?
- Is there an inability to reduce playing or unsuccessful attempts to quit gaming?
- Are they giving up other activities and losing interest in previously enjoyed activities due to gaming?
- Do they continue to game despite problems?
- Are they deceiving family members or others about the amount of time spent on gaming? "Hey, honey, how many hours did you play today?" "Oh, I was only about 30 minutes," and then you get on, seeing that they were on for an hour and a half. "Hey, I sent you to bed at 10 o'clock last night. Did you go to sleep?" "Oh, yeah, I went to sleep," only to find out that after you went to bed at 11, they got back up and played video games from 11:30 until 1:30, and then had to get back up for school the next day.
- Are they relieving negative moods such as guilt or hopelessness with gaming?
- Do they risk jeopardizing or losing their jobs or relationships due to gaming? [10]

That last point actually applies to adults more than teenagers. However, why would adults have gaming disorders? While this book is not about this specific topic, it is interesting to consider that we have more adults playing video games today than ever before. Part of that is because some families are playing video games as a means of entertainment and spending time together. However, psychologists will tell us that adolescence has actually been bumped back into the early 30s. That's in part because these adults are expressing behavior consistent with an adolescent instead of an adult.

Now, do I believe video games are bad? No. I play them; however, I do believe that an adult still needs to be an adult when it comes to their gaming. As a matter of fact, I encourage you to play video games with your kids if they like to play video games. It does a couple of things for you. Number one, it allows you time to connect with your children in something they like, not just in something that you like. And that's big because you chose their turf, which speaks to them. Number two, though, it also allows you to see what they do when they play video games. How aggressive do they get? What words do they use? Do I see a temperament that should cause me concern? It allows you the chance to learn more about your children and gives your child a sense that Mom and Dad want to spend time with them.

Be Aware: Reputation

The last thing I want us to think about is online reputation. And this is not by any means in order of significance. Let's be real. We've already talked about digital footprints and their importance in information harvesting and being used for bad things, but I will also offer this to you. It's also useful when it comes to good things. I came across an example or illustration in my studies: a billboard on the side of a road. The billboard's purpose is to relay information, it is likely to entice you to pull off the road, visit a place, or eat at a restaurant.

Now, some of the best billboards I see are going through Georgia down to Florida. There's a strip there—Tipton, I believe it is—and it's just a row of billboards, probably 50 billboards or more. Usually, half of them are empty or saying "Put your ad here." They also try to draw you to do this by putting "Look!!" on the billboard. You may not think that's a very effective billboard; however, I look. I do so usually because the picture of the cute little dog or the silly face the man is making is interesting. So, there's no doubt that billboards works. They attract the attention of those who drive by.

When I tell you that online reputation matters and the illustration is like that billboard, we need to realize that we all have our own billboard along the information highway if we have a digital footprint. It doesn't matter how old or young you are; you are advertising something to the world. It is interesting to think of individuals who look at your billboard or your children's billboard. The first group that cares about and is concerned about the online reputation of your children is college admissions counselors. If you think for one minute that colleges are not concerned with what your reputation will do to their institution and the community they are trying to build, you are missing the idea of college recruiting. Some admissions advisers check out social media accounts to learn more about the interests of a potential student. Because let's face it, admissions is sales. If they want to connect with somebody, and their social media account reveals this potential student loves hunting, you know what you will talk to them about and make a connection about? Hunting.

You're not going to walk right in and say, "Hey, I've got this great product that you don't have any interest in. Why don't you buy it?" He would look at you and ask, "Why I should buy from you?" You're going to first make a connection, and you're going to connect where they are. What they advertise, that's what people are interested in. Interestingly, more than 80% used social media in the admissions process. More than

80%. So, does it matter what your child posts? Does it matter what your child comments about, what they're looking at, or what others say?

The second category, because it ties in with what other people say about you, is potential employers also look at your digital billboard. Seventy percent of employers use social media to screen candidates before hiring them. Fifty-seven percent are less likely to interview candidates they can't find online. Fifty-four percent have decided not to hire a candidate based on their social media profiles. What are they looking for? Sixty-one percent seek information supporting the applicant's job qualifications, 37% want to know what other people are posting about this particular candidate, and 24% are looking for reasons not to hire the candidate. One out of every four employers who go to social media to find out is looking for reasons why they shouldn't hire your child.[11]

I would love to tell you that your child's digital footprint is inconsequential in the long run, But that isn't the truth. A friend of mine lost his job because of what was posted five years ago on his social media account regarding a developing event in America. He had a confrontation with an individual who was looking for a reason to have a problem with my friend and that person went back into the digital footprint of my friend, and it ended up costing him his job. There was nothing immoral about his posts and nothing that at least half of Americans wouldn't agree with from a political standpoint. Yet he lost his job. This is real—your digital footprint matters.

So now you might be thinking, do I need to go back and delete everything? Do I need to delete everything? Do I need to change everything? Well, here's the problem. You posted something and then you delete it, but what about the friends who copied it and posted it to their page? Or what about they just copied it and saved it somewhere? You can delete it from your page, but that doesn't mean that everybody who's ever posted anything about you will delete it from their page.

You know what? If they tag somebody in that area, they can find out what's happening. I don't even need to go into peers. You understand about reputation and how bullying can occur. We've already discussed cyberbullying, and marring their reputation is definitely a part of that.

I will say this: What can you and I do about their digital billboard? We, as parents and educators, play a crucial role in guiding and shaping their digital behavior. We can teach them three things: conduct, content, and caring. Let me explain what I mean.

- **Conduct**. From the conduct standpoint, we can teach them to be mindful of how they act online. Parents, you and I must be having these conversations with our children. They must be taught to remember that a real person is on the other side of the screen. When a comment is made on social media or by text, it actually impacts people, not computers.

- **Content.** We must intentionally teach our children to think about what they share. Teach them to ask themselves, "Will this embarrass or humiliate me or someone else?" And if whatever you post will bring embarrassment, then don't post it.

- **Caring.** Teach your children to be thoughtful, kind, and caring. Tell them to remember to post with empathy because what they post impacts others. Tell them and show them that social media is a place to share thoughts and opinions, but that as disciples of Jesus Christ, we must never forget to care about the person's soul on the other side of the screen. Teach your children that their purpose, as discussed in an earlier chapter, is to direct people to Jesus, not merely win an argument on social media.

Too many parents have abdicated their responsibility to others when it comes to digital citizenship. That's why I firmly believe schools are teaching this now, because parents aren't teaching it at home, at least not like they should be. I encourage you to reconsider if you're not. You may need to be reminded that it's our responsibility as parents to teach our children digital citizenship.

Conclusion

The evidence is clear that, like a sponge soaked in water, the digital environment in which our children are immersed is shaping their lives in ways that are often unseen but deeply felt. They absorb the values, pressures, and norms of the digital world, and these influences are leading to heightened levels of anxiety, addictive behaviors, and even compromised reputations. The consequences are far-reaching, affecting their immediate happiness, current and future development, and future opportunities. As parents and guardians, we must recognize technology's powerful role in our children's lives and take deliberate, intentional steps to mitigate its potential harms. This could involve setting screen time limits, engaging in open discussions about online safety, and monitoring their online activities. We must become more than passive observers; we must be active participants in guiding our children through the complexities of the digital world.

Guarding the hearts and minds of our children in the digital age requires a multifaceted approach. Monitoring their online activities, making sure the door remains open when it comes to communication, and modeling healthy digital habits ourselves are all incredibly important in this effort. We must teach them to critically weigh the content they consume and share. It's crucial that we help them develop a strong sense of self that is not reliant on the validation of others in the digital world. We also need to encourage them to use technology in ways that build up rather than tear down. By setting clear boundaries and providing the tools necessary for responsible digital citizenship, we can help our children navigate this landscape in a God-honoring manner, with wisdom and resilience.

The task is not easy, but it is essential. The future of our children's well-being highly depends on our ability to intentionally guide them through this digital age with care and deep commitment. Now more than ever, we must be deliberate in protecting their minds and hearts. With the ever-present dangers of digital technology increasing, remember that our involvement as parents can make a significant and positive difference.

5
Social Media

Navigating Social Media as Christian Parents

Social media is an integral part of many of teenagers' lives in today's digital age. As Christian parents, we must grapple with how to help our children navigate this complex landscape. First we must understand that social media, in and of itself, is not inherently evil. It's just a tool; its impact, however, depends on how it is used. As parents, our goal is not to demonize social media. Many of the careers our children will have in the future may require them to know how to use media. That's why we must walk with our teenagers now in how they use it and intentionally teach them to use it wisely, responsibly, and most importantly, in a manner consistent with Biblical principles.

The Role of Social Media in Teenagers' Lives

Social media allows teenagers to express their individuality and creativity. It also serves as an avenue for connectivity, which is crucial in all our lives but especially important in teenagers' lives. Platforms like Instagram, Snapchat, and TikTok, among others, offer the sharing of lives, thoughts, and talents with others. These platforms are often seen as avenues for self-expression and connection, which is why many adolescents are drawn to them. It's also why many adults flock to them and engage in posting and commenting.

Amidst this level of engagement, it's important to acknowledge that social media can enhance our children's communication skills, foster social connections, and even develop their technical skills. These are positive outcomes that should reassure us as parents. However, it's equally important to recognize the potential pitfalls and challenges that come with the territory.

With this in mind, I want to introduce four major social media platforms that young people use today. While you may be familiar with these to some extent, many young people—and possibly many parents—aren't aware of the history behind these social media apps nor are they aware of some of the "behind the scenes" stuff that happens, especially with Snapchat, Instagram, or TikTok.

Snapchat: A Closer Look

Snapchat is one of the most popular social media platforms among teenagers. It's a messaging app that allows users to exchange pictures and videos called "snaps," which are designed to disappear after viewing. The app also includes features like Stories, where users can post content that stays visible for 24 hours, and Snapstreaks, which encourages continuous engagement between users.

While Snapchat might seem like a harmless way to communicate, we need to understand its origins and potential risks. Snapchat was initially conceived in a college dorm room by a young man who, under the influence of marijuana, thought of a way to send disappearing photos—primarily to evade the permanent nature of online content.

The app's initial purpose was to send pictures that wouldn't leave a digital footprint, which could be seen as enabling risky behavior.

One of the significant concerns with Snapchat is the false sense of security it provides. Although snaps are supposed to disappear, recipients can take screenshots, preserving the image indefinitely. This feature can lead to unintended consequences, such as sharing inappropriate content that might resurface later. We as parents must communicate to our teens that once something is shared online, it can potentially exist forever. One way to do this is by having open and honest conversations about the potential risks of social media and by setting clear guidelines for what is and isn't appropriate to share online.

Another aspect of Snapchat that needs to be considered is its business model. Like many other social media platforms, Snapchat is designed to keep users engaged, often through addictive features like Snapstreaks and Maps. The platform's primary goal is to generate revenue through advertising, which means it's in the company's interest to keep users on the app for as long as possible. As parents, we must remind our teens that these platforms are businesses, and their primary objective is not necessarily the well-being of their users. Understanding this business model is crucial in our efforts to guide our children's use of social media.

Instagram: The Allure and the Risks

Instagram, now owned by Facebook (Meta), is another popular platform among teenagers. It allows users to post photos and videos and send direct messages. Instagram also offers features similar to Snapchat, such as Stories and disappearing messages. While Instagram provides a space for creativity and connection, it also presents certain risks of which parents should be aware.

One of the challenges with Instagram is the exposure to inappropriate content. Even if a teenager is not actively seeking such material, the platform's algorithms can sometimes push suggestive or explicit content into their feed. The platform also fosters a culture of comparison. Teenagers are constantly exposed to curated images of others' lives, which can lead to feelings of inadequacy or low self-esteem. It's important to have open, honest discussions with our children about the realities of social media—how what they see is often not a true reflection of real life but a highlight reel carefully crafted to garner likes and followers. This open communication is a powerful tool in our role as guides, empowering us to help our children navigate the digital world with confidence.

TikTok: The Double-Edged Sword

TikTok is a platform that has rapidly gained popularity among young people. It allows users to create and share short videos, often set to music or soundbites. TikTok has become a hub for creativity, with users showcasing their talents, humor, and personalities. However, like Snapchat and Instagram, TikTok comes with its own set of challenges.

One of the primary concerns with TikTok is its origin. The app was developed by a Chinese company, and there have been ongoing concerns about data privacy and security. The Chinese government has different regulations and practices than those in the United States, leading to fears that user data could be shared with the Chinese government. While there have been efforts to regulate TikTok in the U.S., including requiring American companies to invest in the platform, the issue of data privacy remains a concern.

Beyond privacy issues, TikTok also has the potential to expose teenagers to inappropriate content. The platform's algorithm is designed to show users videos that are likely to keep them engaged, which can sometimes mean pushing content that is not age-appropriate. As with other social media platforms, it's essential for parents to monitor their children's use of TikTok and have ongoing conversations about what they are viewing and sharing.

YouTube: The Most Popular and Most Undetected
With over 95% of teens having visited the platform, YouTube reigns as the king of social media sites today. It's a platform that offers a wealth of content, with roughly 75 billion visits per month, second to only Google (who purchased YouTube in 2006), and more than 500 hours of content are uploaded every minute. Users spend on average more than 34 hours per month perusing the offerings to listen to music, watch entertainment content, create and manage personal content, connect with friends, learn new skills, or do educational tasks.[1] This diverse range of content can be a source of learning, entertainment, and connection for your teenager.

While YouTube has many wonderful and beneficial aspects, there are some considerations that parents must be aware of and take very seriously. One of the most popular categories in which many searches would be placed is that of people called influencers or YouTubers. This is so significant because of how easily the adolescent mind can be influenced. When you combine this fact with individuals trying to influence our children for several purposes, we as parents must know what influencers your children are watching. It matters what travel videos, music review videos, and gaming videos your children are watching. It matters because these people are speaking and teaching your children in a way that seems very personal and specific due to the nature of the videos and the plea for interaction in the way of reviews, likes, subscribes, and comments that are left and may be read on the next video by the YouTuber. This influence can also pose potential risks to your child's emotional and psychological well-being.

Understanding the depth of YouTube's influence is crucial. Children often turn to YouTubers to cope with feelings of frustration, loneliness, and boredom. These influencers can shape your child's likes, dislikes, and even their moral and political beliefs. You may notice your child adopting the phrases, interests, or behaviors of their favorite influencers, which highlights the importance of knowing who is influencing your child's life. By understanding and monitoring this influence, you can play an active role in guiding your children's online experiences and ensuring their safety and well-being.

Guiding Principles for Christian Parents

As Christian parents, our goal should not necessarily be to ban social media outright, but to teach our children how to use it in a way that aligns with values and morals taught in God's Word. Here are some guiding principles to help navigate this digital age:

1. **Educate Yourself:** Understand the platforms your children are using. Familiarize yourself with their features, risks, and benefits. This knowledge will empower you to have informed conversations with your children.
2. **Set Boundaries:** Establish clear rules for social media use, such as time limits, privacy settings, and the types of content that are acceptable to share and view. These boundaries should be age-appropriate and evolve as your children grow older.
3. **Promote Open Communication:** Encourage your children to talk to you about their experiences on social media. Create an environment where they can share their concerns, questions, and any negative experiences they might encounter.
4. **Model Responsible Use:** Your children are watching how you use social media. Be a positive role model by demonstrating responsible and respectful online behavior. Show them how to use social media in a way that honors God and reflects Christian values.

5. **Focus on the Heart:** Ultimately, social media is just a tool and the real issue is the heart. Teach your children to seek validation and worth from God, not from likes, followers, or comments. Help them develop a strong sense of identity in Christ, which will guide them in making wise choices online.
6. **Stay Informed:** Social media constantly evolves, and new platforms emerge regularly. Stay informed about the latest trends and potential dangers. This will help you stay ahead of the curve and provide timely guidance to your children.
7. **Pray Together:** Finally, pray with and for your children regarding their use of social media. Ask God for wisdom, protection, and discernment as they navigate this digital world. Encourage them to seek God's guidance in their online interactions.

Conclusion

Social media is an unavoidable part of modern life and can be a powerful tool for connection, creativity, and communication. However, it also presents unique challenges, especially for teenagers. As Christian parents, our responsibility is to guide our children to use social media responsibly, safely, and in accordance with the Word of God. We must continually remind our children of our purpose and mission. We are to be "light" and "salt" that impacts society for the glory of God, even when it comes to the online component of life (Matthew 5:13-16). By educating ourselves, setting boundaries, fostering open communication, and modeling positive behavior, we can help our children navigate the digital age in such a manner that does just that.

6
Digital Leadership

I once read a book by Steve Farrar entitled *Point Man* in which the author emphasizes the importance of male spiritual leadership. Farrar used an extremely impactful opening illustration from the Vietnam War era to underscore his point. Many young men in this time found themselves in extreme hardship in a thick jungle environment where attacks could be unleashed from any direction. The stakes were extremely high, and the costs America paid were great.

Farrar's illustration explains that the soldiers were organized into platoons in the jungle and sent on missions into enemy territory. The enemy knew the terrain well and had already established their presence. The platoons entered the jungle in formations like geese flying in the sky, with the intent being to minimize casualties when an attack was launched against them. They wanted to avoid being grouped because it would make them an easy target for ambush. Each man had to be highly vigilant and keenly aware of their surroundings. Like birds in formation, the soldier at the front, known as the point man, had a unique and challenging role.

In Vietnam, the point man had to be further ahead of the rest of the platoon to listen in the silence for potential threats. He was the first set of ears and eyes when there were boots on the ground regarding what was going on and what was in front of his platoon. He would move ahead of the rest of the platoon to hear any enemy steps or see anything that would cause problems. If a trip line was strung across an opening, it was his job to make sure he saw the line because if he failed, the rest of his platoon would die. And unfortunately many who went into the jungles of Vietnam never came out.

Farrar's illustration is clear. When the point man fails, the platoon suffers. However, when the one who is supposed to be alert, aware, and able to signal to those in his platoon when dangers exist, there is great benefit. Lives can and were saved because the point man was willing and courageous enough to do his job.

The Greatest Influence in Their Lives

I open with that illustration because we've come to the portion of the book that deals with digital leadership. I want you to understand that the consequences and stakes are more significant than merely a physical loss of life. They could impact someone's spiritual walk, family relationships, and the children who have yet to be born. As apostacy has been described numerous times as being only one generation away, the fervor with which we respond to the seemingly overwhelming task before us of helping our platoons, our families, navigate the jungle of technology is consequential.

We aren't talking about a generation who struggles with their faith, purity, self-esteem, or relational expectation. We're describing a scenario where a generation becomes ensnared in a technological trap. Generational consequence continues if we don't get this right.

You may be thinking, "That's a lot of weight to put on the shoulders of families today!" You're right! That is a lot of weight to put on our shoulders. But how would you like me to say it? Would you rather me say, "You know what, if you blow it, who cares? No big deal. No consequence." Or would you rather me speak very plainly? If we fail in our task as parents called not to simply take our children to worship but rather to disciple them in all aspects of life to follow Jesus Christ no matter what distractions may enter the picture, there is the very real potential the chain of faithfulness will be broken.

The reality is that kids raised in the church do fall away. Families that raise children and have close relationships sometimes have children who choose paths the parents didn't want them to take. Therefore, generational consequences come from decisions made when our children are young. This is one of those concepts.

And so, as we begin, I want you to understand that when it comes to digital leadership, there is no more potent example than what you model in front of your children. It's much easier to focus on what Hollywood or Big Tech is doing when it comes to drawing our children into an unrestrained digital demise. However, it gets terribly uncomfortable when we focus on the most crucial influence in the lives of our children—us. Our children are listening to what we say; however, with a greater level of influence, they are watching what we do. They observe our habits when it comes to technology, and often, we see that reflection in their own lives.

Have you ever experienced that? The things that you say, you end up hearing in your children or how you react to stress, you see your children personalizing that. And then suddenly, we have this "Aha moment," and we ask, "Where did that come from? Where did you get that?" And your spouse looks back at you with a hand on the hip and says, "Do you want me to answer that question?" The reason is that you modeled specific responses to them, certain behaviors, and ingrained into them your personal habits. One of the most sobering things about being a parent is that even in our worst moments, we are still teaching them.

My children watch me when I sit in front of a television, relax in a chair, or scroll through my phone. They watch me when I interact with individuals, whether in our family or not. They may think to themselves, "This is how adults are supposed to behave. This is how adults are supposed to interact." That's because as a parent, the example I live before them serves as a model they will frequently follow. Imitating is fundamental to adolescent development, and what you and I model before our children is powerful instruction.

One of the most humbling things that has occurred since becoming a parent over 20 years ago is realizing that I don't only teach when I intend to teach— but that I am constantly teaching. I wish my children only would see when I did well. Wouldn't that be neat? Push the pause button on your kid's paying attention to you. They would only pay attention when I respond to stress nicely and when I deal well with difficulties that might occur in life or when my faith has been challenged because of circumstances. When I'm having a weak moment where I need to cry out, "Lord, I believe, but help me in my unbelief!" (Mark 9:24), I wish I could push the pause button and my kids not see. But here's the truth. I can't, and neither can you. I would even say that it's good for them to see us struggle and continually be drawn closer to God in our walk because in this, we are modeling what it looks like to be continually transformed into who God desires us to become.

There's no doubt that modeling behavior for children has long-lasting effects. That's because we can give them words, but when we give them pictures, it engrains in their mind far more than the words we speak. Think about your family members who have passed from this life. Your grandmother or grandfather may come to mind. There may be a few things that you may remember what they said to you. But you know what you're going to remember? You're going to remember Granny and her kitchen or Grandpa out in the shop. You'll remember the holidays. You won't remember all the conversations, but you'll remember Grandpa, and the smile on his face when he gave Grandma a very special present one Christmas. Why? Because while we don't remember every conversation, we do have images that are ingrained in our minds and those are what stick with us as we mature. A picture is worth 1,000 words, right?

Your interactions are currently being stamped in the minds of your children, for good or bad. It's the verbal and the non-verbal interactions they are filing away. And those memories will be taken into their adulthood. The question is what kind of imprint do you want to leave in their minds?

Modeling Digital Behavior

On average, the current studies say that adults spend 11 hours a day on screens.[1] Some of that is work-related; however, when you consider there are only 24 hours in a day, work related or not, we are spending almost half our time on our devices. Statistics show that approximately one out of every four and almost one out of every three adults say they are constantly online. When compared to the amount of time most adults sleep, exercise, study the Bibles, play games with their children, work, or spend time serving in the ministries of their local congregations, time spent on screens quickly rushes to the top of the list of where time is spent. It's a true statement that as adults, we also have become conditioned to technology, just as our children have.

Sometimes the level of conditioning has gotten so bad that we are much like Pavlov's dog. Remember that experiment? To see how the brain and physical responses can be conditioned, Russian physiologist Ivan Pavlov placed meat before his dog, and every time he did, he would ring a bell, signaling to the dog that dinner was served. He did this for an extended period, until one day, he decided to test the dog's conditioning. He rang the bell but did not put out the meat. The dog still came running, and every time the bell would ring the dog would salivate. Not because there was meat there that he could smell; rather, it was because his brain had been conditioned.

Both we and our children have these have these little devices we carry around and when they "Ding!" just as the bell did for the dog, we immediately reach for them. When it goes off because you've got a message or an email, do we feel this immense responsibility to pick it up and promptly respond? Our reactions to those things play into what we show our children through our modeling. The question is, "What are we truly demonstrating to them in how we respond to media?

Along with this concern regarding what our personal media habits and practices are modeling for our children, I want you to think about the effects your screen time habits are potentially having on your own brain and thus your emotions, memory, stress levels, etc. According to an article written by Mary Grace Descourouez, MS, NBC-HWC, entitled *"What Excessive Screen Time Does to the Adult Brain,"* any amount of time spent on screens outside of work time that exceeds 2 hours per day is excessive. With such usage, the impact is realized in the following ways: eye strain, neck strain, social isolation, and several mental health struggles. The author goes on to report that:

> … increased use of screens among adults may harm learning, memory, and mental health, as well as the potential to increase the risk of early neurodegeneration. The study shows that in adults aged 18–25, excessive screen time causes thinning of the cerebral cortex, the brain's outermost layer responsible for

processing memory and cognitive functions, such as decision-making and problem-solving.

Along with this, the author reports excessive screen time causes:

- Increased risk of developing brain-related disease such as dementia, stroke, or Parkinson's
- Hindering of sleep habits, with the delay of melatonin release from the brain's pineal gland
- Lowering of the gray matter volume, which is essential for daily human functioning such as movement, memory, and emotions[2]

It's difficult for a parent to lead their children in a direction they themselves are not headed. That's one of the most challenging lines you will read in this chapter, and it's challenging because you must pause and consider your own media habits as they relate to where you want your family to go. The statement "Act and speak now as a parent as you want your children to act and speak as adults" is vital to consider. Because frequently, that's what you're going to get. Start asking yourself how do I want my children to act? How do I want them to behave when it comes to social media? What do I want for them when it comes to their spiritual, physical, mental well-being? They're looking for your leadership in this area, and if you lead them toward the trip line or the ambush, you can expect there will be severe consequences. However, if you're aware and alert and leading on this front in what you model before them, there will be great blessing to those in your platoon, both now and as they grow up and leave your house.

What Good Leadership Looks Like

Jesus, at least in His earthly ministry days, seemed to always run into conflict with the Jewish leaders. It didn't matter if He was doing good healing somebody or teaching God's precepts and ordinances. It didn't matter because the Jewish elite had a hierarchy. They had an understanding in their society that they were in charge and waiting for the Messiah, but they did not expect the Messiah to come from a carpenter's son or Nazareth. They were waiting for this grand entry. They had what God was supposed to do in their minds, and they weren't open to what God would do and weren't being aware that since Jesus fulfilled all these Messianic prophecies, maybe they should pay attention to Him. All they were concerned about was He was amassing crowds.

People were going out to hear Him preach. They were going out to be healed. Therefore, they were being pulled away from the Jewish leaders. So the Jewish leaders did not appreciate the ministry of Jesus. They sought to kill Him multiple times, the Bible says, even ultimately culminating in the crucifixion where they used the Roman government to do their dirty work. All of that started because they had rejected Jesus as the Messiah.

John 10 is a passage where Jesus is dealing with that in a very straightforward manner.

> *"Truly, truly, I say to you, he who does not enter by the door into the fold of the sheep, but climbs up some other way, he is a thief and a robber. But he who enters by the door is a shepherd of the sheep. To him the doorkeeper opens, and the sheep hear his voice, and he calls his own sheep by name and leads them out. When he puts forth all his own, he goes ahead of them, and the sheep follow him because they know his voice. A stranger they simply will not follow, but will flee from him, because they do not know the voice of strangers. So Jesus said to them again, "Truly, truly, I say to you, I am the door of the sheep. All who came before Me are thieves and robbers, but the sheep did not hear them. I am the door; if anyone enters through Me, he will be saved, and will go in and out and find pasture. The thief comes*

only to steal and kill and destroy; I came that they may have life, and have it abundantly" (John 10:1-10).

If you highlight in your Bible, you may want to take notice of the different ways Jesus describes Himself. In verses 7 and 9, He says, "I am the door." Then in verses 11 and 14 He describes Himself as "the good shepherd." In both of these, Jesus is teaching a deep principle by drawing a contrast between those who are truly caring leaders and those who are imposters. It's the good shepherd who lays down his life for the sheep (vs. 15, 17, 18). This reality is contrasted with the "hired hand" when in verses 12 -15 He says,

"He who is a hired hand, and not a shepherd, who is not the owner of the sheep, sees the wolf coming, and leaves the sheep and flees, and the wolf snatches them and scatters them. He flees because he is a hired hand and is not concerned about the sheep. I am the good shepherd, and I know My own and My own know Me, even as the Father knows Me and I know the Father; and I lay down My life for the sheep."

The Jewish elite had rejected Jesus. Jesus comes in, and He calls the Jewish elite thieves and robbers with a motive to kill and destroy. Why does He say that? Because they have rejected going through the door. They rejected Jesus. And so He calls them out regarding their motives and the intents of their hearts. Their intent was not to help people get to Heaven. They intended to have sheep follow them, but it was solely for their own benefit, not the sheep's. That's a major contrast here. The good shepherd cares about the benefit of the sheep.

Sheep can graze aimlessly. They can just exist. Why is a shepherd even needed? It's for security; at that time, the sheep would often graze in a paddock or enclosure. That way, they were protected. But the problem is, what happens when somebody jumps over the wall in the back so they can get to the sheep without going through the door?

Jesus as the door—the entrance to the sheep—is drawing a sharp contrast between Himself and the Jewish elite. In trying to jump over the wall, they reveal their sinister motives, which are not for the blessing of the sheep. They were all about appearance and wanted to look and sound righteous before the sheep, with hopes the sheep would empower them by following.

But why would Jesus say He is the door? What's the message He's relaying through this description? If children are playing in a particular area where a gate controls the entrance and the exit, where do parents normally stand or sit? I've seen it numerous times. Parents stand in that opening so that if a child were going to get out of the fence, they would have to get by the parent.

Sometimes my family has been with a big group, especially when our children were smaller. I frequently would walk in the back, and I was that one counting the little ducklings, right? So, if I knew four ducklings were in front of me, I hadn't lost any of them. It was a sense of protection. It gave me the sense that I was in the last line of defense, all because I wanted them to be safe. I wanted them safe for their benefit.

Jesus says in this text that He is the good shepherd. The sheep follow Him because they know His voice. How would the sheep come to know the shepherd's voice? That would only be possible if the shepherd spends time with the sheep. Why don't they know the voice of strangers? Because the strangers are only there for a brief amount of time, and then they're gone again. But the shepherd, the good shepherd, spends time with the sheep. That's why the sheep want to follow the shepherd.

On top of that, Jesus says, look, there's a difference between Myself and the thieves, the Jewish leaders. At the first sign of difficulty, the

Jewish leaders are gone. They're going to leave the sheep out to dry. You know what's going to happen? The wolves are going to come in, and they're going to destroy these sheep because, ultimately, at the end of the day, the leaders weren't about the well-being of the sheep. They were about the well-being of the thieves. Thieves are selfish. They use the sheep for their purpose. But when caring for the sheep will cost them, they are gone. How can you tell the difference between a thief and a good shepherd? Who sticks around when the wolf comes? I don't know how many documentaries you've watched on wolves before, but wolves don't usually travel individually. Wolves hunt in packs. The idea is not that one wolf will take over the sheep; you will have a party of wolves. The difference between the thief and the good shepherd is who sticks around when the wolves come.

I say all that because the Biblical context is this: Jesus is pointing out the difference between Himself and the Jewish elite. He's saying, look, there's a big difference between the Jews who want the sheep to follow them and the good shepherd who wants what's best for the sheep.

While there are so many practical points that could be made from this text, I would like for you to notice some of the concepts about the leadership of Jesus in this case. For us to be good leaders for our families, what are some of the key lessons from Jesus we need to begin implementing if we are not already doing so?

1) Leading My Family Means I Must Lead Them into the Fold (John 10:1-5)

I approach faithful parenting in the digital age from a Christian standpoint. And the fold I'm talking about is this: into the body of Christ. If I am going to lead in the digital age, I cannot pretend to be a leader in my home in only specific categories.

Have you ever noticed people who wanted to compartmentalize their lives? They want to categorize their lives where they will be good in this setting but could be better in that setting. Or they'll be attentive in this format but not attentive in that format. People who tend to want to compartmentalize their lives usually end up with anxiety, depression, and stress, feeling like it's all falling out of control because it's hard to keep so many different plates spinning and remembering what that plate is supposed to mean.

However, could you imagine what your family would be like if you minimized what you were about? What benefits would exist if you narrowed your focus, communicated that focus, and remain committed to that focus? I didn't say simply minimize media usage. There's a much larger concept here, and it's where are you leading your children when it comes to the discussion of eternity.

In the first chapter, we talked about parenting with purpose. We talked about dreaming about what we want for our kids, creating a mission statement, and setting measurable goals to accomplish that concept. What if all your children and grandchildren knew that your entire existence in this world, everything about you, was about bringing honor and glory to God and getting to Heaven? What if your children heard you say that to them? What if your children saw that modeled in your life? What if your children knew that as the father and mother you are willing to stand as the "point man" for your family? And they didn't know it just because you verbally said that. They knew that because they saw that. You were the one who was listening for the enemy. You were the one that was looking for the trip line. You were the one who was ready to give the hand signal for the platoon to stop and seek cover any time you thought you heard something because you were being that attentive.

In 1 Corinthians 11:1, the apostle Paul encouraged the Christians to *"Be imitators of me, just as I also am of Christ."* He was imploring them to watch him in his attitude toward those who were still struggling with the eating of meat sacrificed to idols (8:1-13) and in the way he was focused on bringing as many souls as possible to Jesus to be saved (9:19-27). Ultimately (and this is the reason this text is so challenging) he was saying that by watching him and following in his footsteps, they would also be walking in the footsteps of Jesus because that's where Paul was walking.

This Scripture has become one to which I continually return because it reminds me of the challenge I have as a leader of my family. If we want our children to follow Jesus, the example given is that we as parents must lead them that way. Our leadership must not simply be in putting out a list of rules regarding media usage. Every family needs healthy, God-honoring boundaries when it comes to media, what will be consumed, and how much time will be spent on the devices. However, the leadership we must focus on above all else is leading the hearts of our children to desire to be in a covenant relationship with God through Jesus Christ. That's what will matter in eternity, and that's what will serve as the greatest influence and determinant in the lives of our children as they grow and move away from our homes. We aren't playing the "short game." I encourage you to think down the road and play the "long game." Where do you want your children to be in 20, 30, 50 years? Then lead to that end.

I've got to tell you something. I have failed at that in my life at times. And it hurts. Knowing you've failed hurts because you see it in your kids' lives. That's why I tell you, this is no joke to me; I don't believe it's a joke to you either. The reality is this: if I'm not leading my kids to Heaven, then why would I ever think I can lead them in the digital age regarding what happens with media? Because in everything, I want to be about directing them to Heaven. I will put boundaries in place because Heaven is our goal.

2) Leading My Family Means I Sacrifice for Them (John 10:11-15)

Have you ever checked why you believe your children are valuable? I understand your children are precious; they make you smile and fill your heart with love. I'm not talking about that kind of value. I'm referring to real, tangible value.

There was a time when children were expected to work to help support the family. If you grew up on a farm, you know all too well that it was an all-hands-on-deck concept. You helped bring in the hay. You helped feed for the livestock. You helped when it was time to harvest the chickens—not just get the eggs. If you were too young, you would help get the eggs.

When kids started working outside the house around the turn of the 1900s, they entered the workforce. That was before the 1918 Fair Labor Standards Act, which required minimum wage and hour limits for kids. They would go out, and they would work jobs often in places such as sewing factories where small hands could get into the small places where big hands could not. It is a fascinating cultural study that before World War II, we saw children spending more time around adults than their peers. In these early days of the early 1900s, if a child went off to work, their paycheck would go to help the family—they didn't work to buy the newest $70 video game. And they didn't go to work to buy the newest $100 pair of shoes. They went to work for the betterment of the family. Today, most children would be categorized as consumers not producers. So when I ask about what value they have, now you must assign value on a different level.

Here's the conclusion I've reached. Their value is not based on what they add. Their value is intrinsically placed in their life, not because of what they do but rather because they are created in the image of God (Genesis 1:26-27). Also, they are uniquely valuable to us because, unlike other children, they are ours. That's where their value is rooted. There's a tremendous difference between intrinsic and extrinsic value. Extrinsic value is when they go to work, bring home a paycheck, and contribute to the family. That is an extrinsic value. Intrinsic is why I value them. And because I value them, I will lay down my life for them.

In John 10, Jesus is dealing with a self-righteous group of Jewish leaders who wanted the sheep for irrelevant purposes: political power, personal gain, social status, etc. Jesus wants the sheep because of their intrinsic value. It's this great intrinsic value talked about in Luke 15:1-7 when Jesus describes the great rejoicing in Heaven over one who repents. There's great rejoicing because the soul of that one has a very high value, just as the souls of our children do.

As a leader, I've got to understand and appreciate their value. The reality is this: they are worth everything. They are worth my time, my sleepless nights, my tears, and they are worth whatever financial situation I get myself into to help them because they are more valuable than any of that stuff. Once you understand that you will give everything—time, money, sleep, even your very life— to bring about the well-being of your child's soul, then you begin to understand the value God sees in this text for the sheep.

Based on this same principle, because the souls of my family are so valuable, I will do whatever it takes to protect them from the harms that this digital age may bring. Most people love entertainment, and consequently, will let their guard down as they justify what media they ingest. As a leader in the home we parents must rise above the elementary way of thinking that entertainment is the goal. We must set boundaries that follow Philippians 4:8 and raise our shield of faith to protect the hearts and souls of our children from the flaming arrows of Satan (Ephesians 6:16). Once we decide they are worth it, we will make whatever sacrifices are necessary for their well-being.

3) Leading My Family Means I Know My Sheep (John 10:14, 27)

Jesus says the sheep follow the good shepherd because they know the shepherd's voice. From a leadership perspective, I return to the idea of how the sheep know His voice. The answer is because He spends time with them. Time spent in getting to truly know the sheep and the sheep getting to genuinely know the shepherd adds to the safety and well-being of the sheep.

According to a study published by the U.S. Bureau of Labor Statistics, the average hours parents spend in caring for children and helping with the household is extremely low in my opinion given there are roughly 16 waking hours in a day (not counting 8 hours for sleep). The report claims that the average parent of children 18 years of age and younger spends:

- 1 hour and 24 minutes per day in caring for and helping children
- 32 minutes per day in the physical care of the children
- 2.4 minutes per day reading to/with their children
- 18.6 minutes per day in playing with their children, not counting sports
- 5.4 minutes per day in activities related to household children's educational activities.[3]

Don't miss the decimals in those numbers! When I first saw those numbers, I was shocked. However the more I researched, the more I saw articles about the time that both mothers and fathers spend at work and children spend at school or with extracurricular activities. I read articles about which is better for our children, quality time or quantity time. Both made researched arguments and valid points; however, at the end of the day I keep coming back to a simple principle. My children can't know my voice unless I spend time with them. Not just a few hours a day, but purposeful time and a good amount of it as we walk together and play together.

The cold reality is that our children will know the voices of those whom they spend the most time, be it their peers, other adults, musicians, or any number of other influences. If my voice is going to be the one they hear above all others, then I can't honestly believe that my spending 1 hour and 24 minutes with them every day is going to be enough to stand against the other voices competing with me.

Along with this, we have a lot of family issues in America, even in the church, that make spending time with our children so they know our voices difficult. Divorce and separation occur far too often. Unwed pregnancy is at epidemic levels, and more children live in single parent households today than at any other time in American history. If that's where you find yourself as you read this, please understand, it doesn't mean a cloud of hopelessness surrounds you or your children. While there may be situations in your life that prohibit you spending as much time with your children as you would prefer, in the time you do have with your children, be very intentional. The relationship you develop with your children in times of peace will pay dividends when the wolves of life come.

Sheep recognize a shepherd's voice because he capitalizes on the time he has with them in the peaceful times. Could you imagine if the shepherd was quiet and not engaging with the sheep until the wolf came? Do you think the sheep would suddenly respond to the voice of the shepherd in that scenario? I find it hard to believe they would. It seems like the shepherd has to be very intentional in his interaction with the sheep in peaceful times to make it more likely they would trust his voice in the stressful time.

I've always thought race cars were interesting because of the pit crews. The goal is to spend as little time in the pits as possible. So, when you come into that pit stop, they've got somebody ready to change those tires out, take the screen off the windshield, put gas in the tank, and make that adjustment. They may even have a guy pulling on sheet metal and trying to get it unstuck from the tire. If you need something as a driver, somebody's paying attention to you. But at the end of the day, that pit stop is supposed to be quick. So, you leave because it's hard to come out on top of the race if you stay long in the pit.

One of the best illustrations I have heard regarding how people treat their families is the NASCAR pit stop. We're so busy on the racetrack that the less time we spend at home, the better for our careers. I only come home to get my tires changed and refuel my car, and then I've got to go because if I spend too much time at home, I won't stay caught up. And parents, please listen to this. Your kids need to be more than a pit stop in your life. They need you. If all you've become is a paycheck to your family, that is your fault not theirs. They need you. And they don't just need you there sitting on a chair. Although, that's better than you not being there. They need you to interact with them. If they don't know your voice, they will follow somebody's voice.

4) Leading My Family Means I Must Give Direction (John 10:27)

I love the phrase from John 10:27, *"and they follow Me."* I love this because it summarizes the goal we have for our children, and I'm sure the main goal you have for yours. More than we want our children to get good grades, make the big play in the game, or even get into college, we want them to be a sheep that follows Jesus Christ. If that is their lives' aim and ambition, their media habits and the ways they allow digital technology to influence them will be in its proper place. If that's going to happen, parents must give good directions during the early years of their children's lives.

Have you ever stopped and asked someone for directions? Chances are, even for the toughest man out there, we have all done this at some point in life. Perhaps with the regular integration of Google Maps,

Waze, or Apple Maps we stop less often, but the point can still be made. Complicated directions, or even a lack of clear communication when receiving directions, can make it almost impossible to follow them. That's one of the best things about all the apps that help us navigate. The directions are in writing, we can see a map of where we are going, and there is a voice prompt that makes sure we turn where we're supposed to. At least three different methods of communication are used to help us get to where we are wanting to go.

This same three-fold approach applies when we're talking about leading our families in the digital age in a way that brings honor and glory to God. Jesus directed people to what was written by God, He demonstrated how one was to walk in life, and He verbally taught everywhere He went. The impact of this method is proven. Consider the following.

> **1) Written Directions**—Without a doubt, the importance of leading your family in regular reading and studying God's Word is one, if not the most, important leadership mark you can offer them. It's by reading and studying God's Word they will learn of the nature of God, the nature of His covenants, and what it means to walk with Him versus fighting against Him. With a regular habit of reading the Bible, they will learn of the deep concepts of grace, mercy, repentance, forgiveness, and salvation. They will see that as disciples of Jesus Christ, we really are to live differently from the world around us. They will learn that they have a great purpose as they seek to bring honor and glory to God.
>
> **2) Demonstrated Directions**—I call them the "silent sermons" in life. They aren't the ones that are audible; however, they speak very loudly in our lives. Often, they are much more impactful because there is an image forever etched in our minds by what we see. In the Bible, these directions demonstrated could be when Daniel was

warned not to pray to God but did so any way and then was cast into the den of lions only to be retrieved alive and without any harm (Daniel 6:16-28). These would include accounts such as that of Shadrach, Meshach, and Abednego when the music played, but they did not bow down to Nebuchadnezzar's statue (Daniel 3:1-30). By standing all alone, the three preached one of the most impactful sermons that still resonates with many today, and so will the "silent sermons" you demonstrate before your children as you lead them.

3) Verbalized Directions—There's something extremely powerful about the voice of a parent. From the time before a child is born, through the early years of discovery and exploration, across the years of adolescence, and even through the difficult years of being a teenager, a child who has parents regularly engaging in verbal communication are greatly blessed. In a crowded room or at a busy ball field, when a parent who regularly spends time verbally communicating with their child speaks, the child's brain will recognize the special voice. It's that reality that needs to be leveraged when it comes to parental leadership. Your children need to not only read God's Word and see it lived out in your life, but they also need to hear you explain the direction your family is going and why that is the case. They need to hear why boundaries with technology are good and why following God's Word in dealing with technology is best.

Conclusion

Now, here's the good news. Can a man who struggled as a shepherd of the sheep ever recover? Absolutely! Can a lady who is a shepherd of her home recover if she started on the wrong track? And the answer is resounding "Yes!" Is it easy? No. The reason it's not easy is because your kids cannot unsee or unhear what they have already seen and heard. But does that mean that you cannot change it? You absolutely can, and you absolutely must.

It would help if you considered the lessons from John 10. Here's why. At the end of the day, the hearts of your spouse and children are the most important entities in your home. The Bible says that we need to watch over and guard our hearts because the springs of life flow from them (Proverbs 4:23). Why is it that we act the way we do, talk the way we talk, and have or not have a dedication to God? It's not merely an obedience issue. It's a heart issue.

I served as a preacher at a congregation and was asked to visit a brother in Christ who had stopped coming to services. The goal was simple. We wanted him to come back and regularly attend. And I was relatively new as their preacher then. And another brother said, "Hey, I'm going to visit him. Would you come with us?" And I said, "I'll go with you" and talk to this fellow who had been absent from worship. He had struggled with drugs and alcohol. It wasn't just that he wasn't coming; he had walked a long road.

When we arrived to his house, he let us in, and it was a very nice visit. As we were talking about why we were there, this other brother said, "Hey, we want to invite you to come back to the church. We miss you. We want you to be there." And this gentleman said, "Well, here's my rule. I'll come any time somebody asks me." Many might be tempted to think that's a great attitude. After all, he'll come when somebody asks. I hear things differently sometimes. What I heard was, "I'll go because you asked, not because I want to be there." And so, when it came time for me to speak, I said, "I'm not going to ask you to come back to services—I'm going to ask you to reengage as a disciple of Jesus Christ."

Why did I do that?

If he reengages as a disciple of Jesus, his attendance will take care of itself. Attendance is an outflow, an overflow. Your worship is not a marker of faithfulness. Your worship is an overflow that comes because you already are faithful. Being in a building is not enough to make one a disciple of Jesus Christ. There must be an internal change—a transformation—that causes that individual to want to gather with the assembled saints and praise God. There's a big difference between the person who attends because someone asked them to do so and someone who can't wait to be there because God is that special and that important in their lives.

Remember, as parents, the goal is not to raise "church attenders." Rather, we are to raise up a generation who are true disciples of Jesus Christ in every meaning of the word. Our aim is to shape the hearts of our children so that they make the choice to continue in the Word of God (John 8: 31-32). If we want them to study the Way, know the Way, and go the Way, we must be out in front of them leading them in the Way (see John 14:6). However, it's not just about what they know. It's whether what they know has saturated their heads to the point where their hearts are soaked with the Word of God. We want them to love God with all their heart, soul, mind, and strength, and love their neighbors as themselves (Mark 12:30). We want their lives to be a living sacrifice to the glory of God (1 Peter 2: 4-12), and we want their declaration of their love for God not to be merely verbal but also active (John 14:15).

Ultimately, it's not about whether your children view pornography. I'm concerned with that, but that's not where this is going. It's not whether they play video games, use their cell phones all the time, don't sleep enough, or have behavior issues like not remembering things or being irritable. This entire book would be useless if it were only about setting boundaries to modify the behavior of your children in relation to digital media.

Here's why. I can threaten my children enough that they are obedient to me, but that doesn't mean there's been any change in their lives. One day they're going to be out of our house; I want them to make the right decisions then. Ultimately, I want their heart to be won over to the Lord. That's what this book is about. Reaching the hearts of our children, not just putting up rules.

I don't know how reading this chapter hits you. Some of you may be thinking, "We're doing some really good things at our house. You know, we've got all these things in line." Here's what I want the challenge to be. Dads, I'm speaking to you men first and foremost because you set the pace. Have you been standing point in your family? Or have you just been existing? Brothers, one of the worst things you can do is just turn this page while either refusing to evaluate where you are, or worse, lying to God. So, I'll ask the question again. Have you been standing point in your family?

Men, we've got to stand point. We've got to be the ones that stand up. We've got to take the lessons from the Shepherd. Men, if it doesn't start with us, who does it begin with?

Ladies, let me ask you a question. Your impact on the children, especially the younger ones, is so significant that it drives their personalities and responses to many stimuli and concepts. Mothers impact the lives of their children in ways that fathers never can. So, mothers, let me ask you a question. Have you been standing point in your homes? If not, who are you waiting on? You say, "My husband. I'm waiting for my husband to do it."

I would love to have your husband do it, but what if your husband doesn't? Do you throw your hands up and say, "Well, there's a trip line right there. My husband should warn us about it. I see it, but I'm just not going to say anything." I know you would speak up, especially if you knew the lives of your husband and children depended on it. So, let me ask you a question. How have you been doing? Now, here's the challenging part. Most adults can lie to themselves pretty quickly, justify what they're doing, and say, "I'm doing enough."

Let me ask a question. What would your children and grandchildren say if I asked them how you're doing? Do you want to know how they might answer that?

I'll give you a couple of questions.

- When was the last time you led your family in Bible study at home?
- When was the last time you sat down and talked with your family about why you don't watch certain TV shows?
- What limits have you set on the internet, and what boundaries have you enforced?
- When was the last time you sat and prayed with your family about the attacks of Satan and asked that God would guard you?
- When was the last time your children heard you pray at all, outside of meal times?

Your answer is probably much like mine, at times in my life—not near enough. The goal is not for you to read another book that makes you feel bad about your parenting skills. If that's all this is then you might as well put it down and move on. This is about reaching your heart so you will guard the hearts of your children. It's very possible that the answer to the pitfalls of digital media in your home begin with you and your relationship with God. What if your family rededicated themselves to God today? What would be different in your home?

I encourage you not to let Satan steal this moment of reflection. He would love nothing more for you to tune out and move on as if you never read this chapter.

7
When the Ambulance Is Necessary

What do you do when things have started going down a difficult path? This question stems from a conversation I had with a gentleman who attended one of my seminars. He said, "Joe, not everyone attending your seminars will be young parents with children still in diapers or who haven't started a family. Some may have grown children who are struggling. Others may have teenagers, and after attending your seminar on digital parenting, they might decide to make some changes at home. But those teenagers might react negatively and say, 'Whoa, we don't like Joe at all because of what he told our parents!' So, what do you do then?" That's a very valid point, so this chapter addresses that genuine concern for parents of older teens who may just now be considering the principles in this book for the first time.

I ask you to imagine a guardrail. Guardrails serve a purpose—they mark the edge of safety. You'll notice that guardrails are installed in the "safe zone," typically at the top of a ditch, not at the bottom. A guardrail at the bottom of the ditch is useless because the car has already gone off the road before there's contact with the guardrail. Thus, they are installed at the top of the ditch, in the "safe zone," so if the car begins to veer off the road, the guardrail will hopefully serve as a boundary to keep the vehicle away from more significant danger. The purpose of a guardrail is to keep vehicles within the bounds of safety.

Now, let's consider an ambulance. Ambulances are known for responding to people in need, those who are hurt and need to get to the hospital quickly. They provide immediate first-responder treatment until the patient can receive better care at the hospital. The ambulance serves a purpose because someone is injured.

Let me ask you a question. Here's the illustration: would you rather have guardrails at the top of a cliff or an ambulance at the bottom? If you could only choose one, which would you prefer? Of course, you'd select the guardrails. The reason is simple: We don't even want to imagine needing the ambulance at the bottom of the cliff. It's much easier and saves a lot of trouble when you have the guardrails at the top.

But the reality is that not everyone is in a situation where their life has had guardrails. Some families have yet to put them in place. Nowadays, there is no good excuse not to have some sort of filtering on your home internet. There just is no good excuse. If you tell me, "Well, I just haven't gotten around to it," then the reality is that's not a good excuse. If you tell me it costs money, I can show you options that cost very little and some that are free. If you say, "Well, then I can't search the internet like I want," that's a horrible excuse, too, because the things you don't need to see are what's being filtered out, and you can change the settings based on whether it's for adults, teens, or kids.

Why do I say that? Because some people will read this and not make any changes. Nothing makes them say, "Oh, maybe we need to go home and take this more seriously." That's when dangers occur, that's when addictions take hold, that's when anxiety levels spike and frustration and impulses are not controlled. That's when fits are thrown, words are screamed, relationships are damaged, and, more importantly, individuals are more concerned about what video game they will play instead of asking, "Did I worship God with all of my heart this morning?"

Even with guardrails you still may end up needing an ambulance. The good news is that there's still hope for recovery. There's always good news in this. I've had people in my seminars who would come up to me and say, "Well, I wish I had heard that when my children were growing up." I've had parents, through tears, sit down in the back of an auditorium or pull me aside in a foyer to share how they raised their children, and now that their children are grown, they see how their actions directly impacted their children's lack of faithfulness. You can feel their pain as you see the hurt stream from their eyes.

And here's what I tell them: As long as there's breath in your lungs, and as long as there's breath in your children's lungs, there's hope. There's hope. You don't stop being a parent when your kids leave the house, whether at 18 or 30 or whatever the average age is today, right? You're always a parent, and your influence is always there. It's never too late.

But often, it must begin with a step, and that step can be very painful. If we're going to understand the impact of this ambulance at the bottom of the cliff, then we've got to take ownership of why our loved one went off the cliff in the first place as much as we can. Please understand, they're not robots. The book of Ezekiel tells us that the one who sins will be accountable for their sins (Ezekiel 18:4). A son will not be held accountable for the father's sins. The father will not be held accountable before God for the son's sins, but the one who sins will be accountable. As much as I don't want my children to walk away from the Lord, if they choose to do so I am not accountable to God for their decisions, but I am responsible to God for what I did or did not do that influenced them. They get to make their own decisions. Parents tell me, "Joe, we brought our kids to the church building every time the doors were open, and they're still not faithful." And I ask them, "How much a part of your life was God every other day of the week besides Sunday and Wednesday night? What impact did He have on Monday in your home? What impact did He have on your home on Tuesday? Or Thursday, Friday, Saturday?" Often, you find out they believed that if they brought their kids to the building, faithfulness would happen automatically because they were at the church building. The reality is you can't get your kids to the church building enough.

Think about that. Two hours on Sunday morning, one hour on Sunday night, one hour on Wednesday night, and let's throw in a youth event just to give us an extra buffer. That's five hours a week if that's all you do for your children in their walk with the Lord. They get more screen time in one day than they would get in the study of God's Word in an entire week. You'll never overcome it that way. That's why the home must be where this is done.

Some parents hear this and say, "Well, Joe, I can look back now and reflect on what happened." And I would say this: It's okay to take ownership, but you will not be held accountable for what your sons or daughters did. You will have to live with what happened and what you did or did not do. Now, here's what I mean by saying it's difficult, because it's forgiveness. To recover from this, you've got to forgive yourself. And that's hard if you don't believe God can forgive you.
Here's what I know about God. God is in the forgiving business. He's in the restoration business. You ask what God's all about—I know you know the answer to this—God sent His Son to die on this earth and to resurrect Him from the grave because He's in the restoration business. He wants to restore relationships. He didn't wait on you and me to first love Him; He sent Jesus to the earth because He loved us first, and He sent Jesus to die on the cross for those who were helpless and those who were his enemies, those who were sinners (Romans 5).

Can God forgive you if things you did as parents may have contributed to your children's problems? Maybe your lack of involvement or lackadaisical approach has had ramificiations? Maybe your realize that events occurred in your family and you need to take ownership? It's important that you understand and take ownership. But it is even more important that you understand we serve a God who forgives! Don't lose sight of that fact. You can be forgiven, and your children can be forgiven!

See, the things we've addressed in this book have not even gone into depth about the sinful practices that happen with the Internet. We haven't gone into depth on the topic of sexting, where individuals will send inappropriate messages or pictures over the phone, over video game chat sites, or social media. We just barely touched that. We didn't delve deeply with pornographic addictions, although we did touch the subject of pornography and how individuals get drawn into that, and before too long, it entangles them more and more in a world that now they don't know how to get out of it.

With all the pitfalls and traps Satan is using when it comes to digital media, sometimes teenagers who falter get caught in the sense of, "Well, I'm just horrible. God can't forgive me for this." What I want you to hear is this: God is in the restoration business. He can forgive. Interestingly, when I study this subject, I look at passages like 2 Samuel 11 with David and Bathsheba. King David takes another man's wife, and then he has that man killed. God sends a speaker, a prophet named Nathan, to tell David a parable about a rich man who took a poor man's ewe lamb when the rich man could have taken one of his many lambs, but he didn't. He took that one man's lamb. David gets upset about it. He gets fired up. And Nathan looks back at him and says, *"You are the man"* (2 Samuel 12:7).

David is convicted. David is shattered for the first time in that whole process. His greatest sorrow is sinning against God. We know he mourns for the child conceived by his horrendous actions. And we know once the child passes, he takes off his clothes of mourning and he moves forward. That's where you hear, *"I will go to him, but he will not return to me"* (2 Samuel 12:23). In his great sorrow, David writes Psalm 51, which expresses powerful concepts of restoration and a sincere desire to be right with God.

> *"Be gracious to me, O God, according to your loving kindness, according to the greatness of your compassion. Blot out my transgression, wash me thoroughly from my iniquity, and cleanse me from my sin"* (Psalm 51:1-2).

The internal struggle is terrible as he writes, *"For I know my transgressions and my sin is ever before me"* (Psalm 51:3).

Have you ever felt that way when it seemed you couldn't escape your past? I've known individuals who define themselves by their past. They struggle and tell themselves, "I can't ever see myself as anything other than an addict." "I don't see myself as anything other than a person who cheated on my spouse." "I don't see myself as anybody other than someone fired from that job because of a lack of integrity. I can't see anything beyond my failures." And David relates when he says, *"My transgression is ever before me"* (Psalm 51:3).

I love concepts that bring to light more extensive illustrations. Think about this. I've never worked with stained glass, but I know that one of the methods has to do with breaking a pane of glass already there so that you can piece together the parts to make the beautiful stained glass. Perhaps you've done this. Once each piece is placed in just the right place by the master artist, you see the beauty of the variations of color. Once a pane of stained glass is broken, the pieces, most of which would be cast aside by the untrained eye, can be positioned in a useful and beautiful manner. However, it all begins with brokenness.

When an individual sins, it requires brokenness before God will create beauty again. God's capable of forgiveness and able to restore, but see here's the deal. For the person who never asks for forgiveness, who never seeks forgiveness, who never comes back to Him, all you're really going to be is shattered glass on the floor.

But there's good news! When an individual repents and comes to God with a broken and contrite heart or a contrite spirit (Psalm 51:17), God is willing and able to piece together what was once broken into something beautiful and valuable for His purpose. The stained glass reminds me of this: What once was broken can be made beautiful again. As God promised His people through the prophet Isaiah, He will give the afflicted *"a garland instead of ashes"* and *"the oil of gladness instead of mourning"* (Isaiah 61:1-3). Joy is possible, even after failure has occurred.

This is where we begin in dealing with the topic of recovery. I don't recover by pretending like nothing ever happened. The ambulance was there. My loved one, my child, my spouse, myself, whoever it is—the ambulance is necessary because we didn't put guardrails up top. But I want you to know this: God can take what was broken and make it beautiful.

What do you do? It's never too late to put up the guardrail. You say, "Joe, my kids are teens; we've gone so far down this now it's just become a regular practice." And I would offer this to you: That may be the case, and I'm not suggesting that this will be easy because it won't. When you start enacting rules and setting boundaries that weren't there in the first place, you can expect teens not to appreciate that. And you can expect your own inconvenience.

If your rule in your house is no social media or no devices after 9:30 at night because you want them to have 30 minutes of downtime so they don't have the blue light impacting their brains, making it difficult for them to get into deep sleep, and you say no devices after 9:30 p.m., guess who needs to put their device down at 9:30 as well? You do. Again, this goes back to the modeling concept. You can say certain things, but if your kids see you model something different, it will have a detrimental impact on their lives.

Suppose you're one of the parents who has been more lackadaisical, an individual not necessarily strict, and you've been hands-off. Boundaries haven't really been a part of your parenting style. In that case, I need you to know something: God is the originator of boundaries. The concept of boundaries is God's idea. Is it possible that God knows when boundaries exist, then people have more security and safety? When I look at Exodus 19:12, the Bible talks about Moses going up on Mount Sinai, and the children of God, the Hebrews, were not supposed to get on or even close to the mountain. The Bible reads, *"You shall set bounds for the people all around, saying, 'Beware that you do not go up on the mountain or touch the border of it. Whoever touches the mountain shall surely be put to death.'"* And you may look at that and say, "Joe, that just sounds like God wasn't being necessarily nice because, after all, who cares if they touched the mountain?" God did.

And here's what we need to understand about God and how that plays into parenting: God sets boundaries because He knows what's beneficial for His people. He also sets boundaries because He knows that if boundaries don't exist, people will treat Him as if He were unholy, regular, or just like every other authority. The boundary is in place because this was a unique, holy concept; therefore, it is in place so the people would recognize God as holy in their lives.

Think about that. God is the originator of boundaries. Psalm 74:17 says: *"You have established all the boundaries of the earth; you have created summer and winter."* In Ephesians 6:1, the apostle Paul addresses this concept of boundaries by pinpointing the responsibility of obedience and adherence to the boundaries within the home. *"Children obey your parents in the Lord, for this is right."* How can children obey parents if parents don't have boundaries? You've got to have boundaries. And then you've got to hold people accountable.

Can you imagine a boundary that exists—a rule that is given—but never enforced? It's mind-boggling that laws exist—some are enforced, and some are not. You know what? A law that is not enforced is not really a law. A law is only good if somebody will implement punishment when the law is transgressed. So parents, when you tell your children the rules, you need to love them enough to enforce them—not because you're evil, but because you love them. The proverb writer in Proverbs 3:12 said, *"For whom the Lord loves, he disciplines just as a father disciplines the son in whom he delights."*

When I was in college, still at home with my parents, they were house parents at a children's home. This home was a place for children ages 13-18 to go just before juvenile hall. For most, those who were placed there had been taken away from their parents because they did something violent or because their parents had not been good parents. I could tell stories about children who had cigarette butts put out on their arms, moms who chose boyfriends over their own children, and parents who invited friends in to take advantage of their children. All kinds of stories that were horrendous and would break your heart.

What's sad is when you consider what these boys came out of and why they came to us in the first place, I can completely understand why they felt the way they did and thus acted with such disregard for authority. However, in a six to eight-month period of time, we tried to take them from a rebellious individual to being people who willfully obeyed as they worked the program so that they could get out and live productive lives within society.

When they first came in, you know what we did? If they came in with hair that was out of control, one of the first things that we did was cut their hair. What happens when you go into the military? One of the first things they do to all males is shave their heads. When these boys came into the home, they were each given a uniform. All of them had khaki pants, the same color. They either had a yellow shirt, a brown shirt, or a green shirt, each representing different program levels.

We also gave them something else. Have you ever seen those Scout-type belts, the web belts you pull through, and then you move that little slide, and it locks it in? What did we do to keep them from sagging their pants? We had them pull the pants up above their hips to just below their belly button or right at their belly button, made them cinch one of those belts down, and then we took scissors and cut the rest of the belt off so they couldn't loosen it.

There were penalties if they showed up out of uniform. They woke up in the morning, and they had zero privileges. They had to earn every one of those privileges. We had an on-campus school they had to attend. They had to be in uniform, turn everything in, and be respectful. If they did all of that, then they would get to watch TV for about 30 minutes.

You might look at that and say that's just horrible. But you know what we found? The kids who came in from an unstructured environment lived in our structured environment, and in six to eight months, they were almost like different kids because kids function well when there are limits. Kids function well when there are boundaries. We used to say it this way: A kid who doesn't know where the boundary ends will be a kid who keeps running all over. A kid placed within a boundary area will run into the wall until he says, "Oh, there's a wall there. I don't want to keep running into that." Then he'll run into that wall, then he'll run into this one, then he'll run into that one. He will try the walls to see if they're stable.

Guess what happens, though, once he realizes all those walls will stand? He will function more peacefully because he knows those boundaries protect him. Boundaries are a blessing and contribute to positive mental peace.

Have you ever thought about that? Telling your child that she cannot be on the cell phone or that he can't be on the game system all the time will allow them to have more peace. They won't like it at first. The kid in the ambulance hypothetically will not like it initially, but it will be best for him.

We've talked about repentance and forgiveness, and we've talked about boundaries. The last thing I want us to talk about is this: How do you help? After studying everything I've looked at—the medical journals, the psychology reports, and everything that we've gone through—I am convinced that a lot of the issues that we see with young people center around self-esteem and self-worth. It also centers around the subject of identity. In other words, kids are in a state where they are searching for their identity. Who am I? Where do I fit in? Will people like me? Will I be accepted? Am I worth loving? Am I not worth loving? And all of has to be answered as they develop.

We've got to understand that if we're going to help that young person who needed the ambulance to get out of the ambulance, to recover, then we've got to deal with self-worth, self-esteem, and identity. The reality is this: Adolescence is an interesting period, and I equate it to going through one of those funny mirror houses at a carnival. I don't know if you've ever been through there. There are mirrors that change your appearance in all kinds of ways. I love the mirrors that make you look skinny, right? So I may stand in front of one of those mirrors more than the ones that make you look a different way. But if you've ever been in front of those, you're like, "Ooh, I like the way I look in this one." Remember, just because the mirror reflects it doesn't mean it's what you really look like.

When young people spend all their time looking into the mirror of culture and allowing culture to tell them what they look like, they will get a skewed view of what they truly are. And when you and I spend all our time hoping other people will affirm us and tell us we are valuable, we will always come up short because it will always be based upon what other people think of us. In terms of adolescents, they are continually trying to reach out and discover who they are. One of the ways that they'll reach out to find out who they are is through family relationships. In other words, I am the youngest child; therefore, I identify as the baby, and I will always act like the baby of the family. Or, perhaps they think, "I am the oldest in the family; therefore, I will always act like the oldest. That is my identity."

Others will look for identity through status symbols. This identity is based on what I have and what I don't have. When I travel and speak to teens, I bring my old high school letterman jacket for one of my lessons. I still have it, and it still fits and has all the pins on it from when I lettered. I was a three-year letterman in track and football, the state or district championships we won. I was a captain of the team. I even have a little pin from the eighth grade to prove I was on the team. The idea is this: I bring that coat to the lesson and put it on. It kind of feels good, quite honestly, to put my high school jacket on. I put it on and start telling the kids about everything I used to be. It may surprise you. I was the president of the senior class, the president of the National Honor Society, and the president of the National Junior Honor Society. I was the Snowball King. That's a true story. My crown was a Wal-Mart Santa hat. I was a football team captain in my eighth-grade year and again my senior year. I made All District. I was somebody at one time. Can you imagine, though, if I let who I used to be define my identity today? Have you ever met one of those guys? They don't know how to move on from their high school days. All they are, their worth, is what they've accomplished and what they used to be. Can you imagine a man who only ties his self-worth to whether or not he has that car, whether or not he has that house, or whether or not he's accomplished what other people consider success? That's what sometimes kids do. And occasionally, big kids do the same thing.

Another source of identity for teens is through grown-up behavior. Young people associate participating in grown-up behavior as being more mature or rebelling (as if that was what was supposed to happen) against the values of their families or the school or society or what was taught in God's Word. They get their identity from being a rebel. Others will search for their identity in others' opinions of them or through idols such as Hollywood or music stars. And some even get their identity through cliquish exclusions. In other words, I'm a part of the group; if I'm a part of the group, that means I'm somebody.

The problem is it's all a facade. When they are hunting for identities in those false things, they will never get to the root of where their identity comes from. They will only have an identity rooted in what other people think about them. Let's translate that concept generically about adolescents to the digital world. Why do they care if people like their posts? Why do they care if people share or comment on their posts? Why do they care if people go to the mall without them or go to watch a movie without them? Great for them, right? Who cares if I was left out? Do you know why that's always a big deal? Because they believe who they are is who they see through the lens of their interactions with the digital world.

So when somebody on that video game site doesn't know who I am, but they know my gamer name, and they start talking smack about me and degrading me through my gamer name, even though they don't know my name, I take that personally. Then it starts to hurt because other people don't think I am very good at this game. I go into chat sites that the gamers go to, and I see people using derogatory terms about me. Why is it that it starts to hurt me? See, the reality is, adults understand that are real friends and then online friends, which are two separate categories. Kids don't view life that way. To them, it's the same. Imagine people saying derogatory things about them in real life or leaving them out in real life. That's the way the digital world impacts our kids.

Really, it's the same issue that's been going on for generations. It's not like today's generation just wants to be liked, while back in the day, they didn't want to be liked. Adolescents have always gone through this. Now when it expresses itself, the playground is the digital medium. What do we do? How do we help the children that get wrapped up in this and land in the ambulance? We've got to let them see that their identity is not rooted in what other people think of them.

Instead, we've got to let them see that their identity is rooted in the fact that God created them. Their value is not because someone else places value on them. Their value is because God placed value within them. He powerfully expressed this tremendous value when He sent His Son to die on the cross. They weren't deserving of such a sacrifice anymore than we are. However, in so doing, God demonstrated, in a very meaningful way, the value He has placed upon all of us.

If young people are reading this, please listen to me. You are unique! In all of creation, there is only one created thing that is said to be made in His image—humanity. That means that He placed within you a soul that will live for eternity—and He wants your soul to live with Him! Your soul is who you are. Your body is an external shell. Who you are is what lives on for eternity. That is rooted in the fact that you are made in His image. And no matter who bad-mouths you on social media, it doesn't change that God created you in His image. Whether they invite you to the party or not, whether they talk about you on social media or like your posts, it doesn't matter because you matter to God. God made you in His image.

When we begin rooting our children not in what they accomplish or what they have but instead root them in God, that is the only constant they need in this world. Did you hear me say that? You and I will eventually graduate from this life into eternity, most likely, leaving our children on this earth. There's no way for us to know how everything's going to work out in their lives after we leave. We don't know what's going to happen in their marriages. We don't know what's going to happen in their jobs. Will they be successful as man determines success, or will hardships of life come upon them? We just can't know; however, we do know this: God is the constant in their lives that will never change. He will always, always love them. When you begin to root your children's identity and self-worth in what lasts, they will be more resilient in dealing with what happens in the digital world.

Our identity is recognized as being made in His image. You're the only part of the creation that was made in His image and has a soul. But you also have another ability: You can reason. Animals don't have the ability to reason. They operate on instinct, yet you can reason. In Isaiah 1:18, God called Israel to Himself to reason together. It never says that He called the trees to reason with Him or the lions to reason with Him. The bears don't reason to go into hibernation; they do that by instinct. Some animals may eat their young because it's how they were made. It's not reasonable.

You can make choices. You have a sense of morality and justice. They call that moral oughtness. You can be self-aware. You have a sense of the eternal. When I say self-aware, it means that gorillas don't sit around and say, "I wonder what it means to be a gorilla?" Or a cat sit around and think, "I wonder what it means to be a cat?" Or grass sit around and say, "I wonder what it means to be grass?" Humans have the ability to be self-aware. David would ask in Psalm 8:4, *"What is man?"* That's a question to ponder about self-awareness. Who are we?

I want you to remember that our identity and your children's identity are grounded in the fact that from birth, we're image bearers of God. Even when sin overtakes us (Romans 3:23), because of God's grace and mercy, through obedience to the gospel, we put on the new self of Ephesians chapter 4 and Colossians chapter 3. The old is removed and we are clothed in the new. What does the new look like? The new is what God has redeemed us to be. That's the pureness, the sinlessness. That's the idea of holiness. If I continue to walk in the light as He is in the light, the blood of His Son, Jesus, continually cleanses me from all my sins (1 John 1). As we were initially created in His image, we can be made new through the blood of His precious Son, Jesus Christ.

That doesn't mean I can't fall away. Galatians 5 teaches that I can be cut off from grace. But what I have in the book of 1 John is an assurance that if I continue to walk in the light, I don't have to live life looking over my shoulder. God doesn't say He will forgive you only to turn around and make you wonder if you were going to Heaven. That's why 1 John says we can know we have eternal life. Why can I do that? Here's what I have to realize: I became an image bearer of God when I became a Christian. I recognize that I'm created in His image, and I'm rooted in the fact that I'm created in His image.

You say, well, how does that help children? It helps young people because when you think of all the things that they're going to encounter and have encountered in their digital imprint—the cyberbullying that maybe some have experienced, sexting, pornography, video game usage, all of that—it still comes back to the heart. If I want to reach my kid's heart, I've got to tie their heart to God in every way, shape, and form, including their identity.

How do I do that? Again I go back to this, and I won't belabor it because I've brought it up before. There is nothing that replaces your presence in their life. Nothing. You can't say they have the greatest teachers in school and they replace the children's need for me. No. They can have some of the most outstanding teachers, but those teachers will never be Mom or Dad. Well, you say, they've got good friends. That's great, but those friends can never be Mom or Dad. If you seek to be your kids' friends, who will be their parents?

You say, "But Joe, you can be both!" They need friends and they have friends, but they need parents, and those are not always friends. Do you know why? Because you demand respect, you demand obedience to the boundaries that you've set. The goal is that as they grow, our children become our friends, and then we guide them, not threaten or command them.

This is where we are in our family. I would love to tell you I'm ready for it. I don't know how ready I am. But I do know this: I feel very blessed to be a father and a husband and have the opportunity to parent faithfully, even in a digital age. There's a part of me that would love to return to before computers existed. But you know what I'd find? I would still find a need to be faithful in parenting within that context. This book would read a little differently in the mediums I discuss; however, the basic principles have never changed. So don't think that you're not equipped. You are absolutely equipped.

You say, "Well, I'm not up on all things technology." That's okay because as soon as you think you've got it, it's like grabbing a handful of water from a river. You pull it up and say, "Aha, I have what's current, and I know what's going on." Guess what happened to the place where you got that water from? It's already gone downstream. It's already old news when you grab it out of the river because new water has flowed down. That's the way this subject is.

Conclusion

As we approach parenting faithfully in the digital age, just be aware: It's always better to have guardrails on the top of the cliff, but sometimes the ambulance is necessary. Sometimes, we, and possibly our children, have gone over the safe area, and injury has occurred. Recovery is possible and available. God is in the restoration business. He is in the forgiving business. He can handle whatever we've done. God can take our broken pieces and remake us. He desires a broken and contrite spirit. If you allow sin to convict you, He can remake you into a beautiful mosaic-stained glass. He does that through the blood of His Son, Jesus. Today, maybe that's where you are. Healing begins with you coming to Him. It starts with you recognizing what sin has done in your life. Begin with realizing that God needs to once again be the center of your life and your home.

Connect Them To Jesus

End Notes

Chapter 1

1. "Accidental." *Merriam-Webster.com Dictionary*, Merriam-Webster, https://www.merriam-webster.com/dictionary/accidental. Accessed 21 Mar. 2022.
2. "Purpose." *Merriam-Webster.com Dictionary*, Merriam-Webster, https://www.merriam webster.com/dictionary/purpose. Accessed 21 Mar. 2022.
3. Ramsey, Dave. *Entreleadership: 20 Years of Practical Business Wisdom from the Trenches.* Howard Books, 2011. pp. 34–38.
4. https://www.goodreads.com/author/quotes/4918776.Seneca.

Chapter 2

1. Common Sense Media, "The Common Sense Census: Media Use By Kids Age Zero to Eight." 2020.
2. Rideout V, Peebles A, Mann S, & Robb MB. *Common Sense Census: Media Use by Tweens and Teens.* San Francisco, CA: Common Sense. 2021.
3. Radesky, J., Weeks, H.M., Schaller, A., Robb, M., Mann, S., and Lenhart, A. *Constant Companion: A Week in the Life of a Young Person's Smartphone Use.* San Francisco, CA: Common Sense. 2023.
4. Rideout V, Peebles A, Mann S, & Robb MB. *Common Sense Census: Media Use by Tweens and Teens.* San Francisco, CA: Common Sense. 2021.
5. American Psychological Association. "Teens Are Spending Nearly 5 hours Daily on Social Media. Here Are the Mental Health Outcomes." *Monitor on Psychology*, 55(3). April 1, 2024. https://www.apa.org/monitor/2024/04/teen-social-use-mental-health.
6. Radesky, J., Weeks, H.M., Schaller, A., Robb, M., Mann, S., and Lenhart, A. *Constant Companion: A Week in the Life of a Young Person's Smartphone Use.* San Francisco, CA: Common Sense. 2023.

7. "Teens and Internet, Device Access Fact Sheet." Pew Research Center, *Pew Research Center*, 5 Jan. 2024, www.pewresearch.org/internet/fact-sheet/teens-and-internet-device-access-fact-sheet.
8. Twenge, Jean M. "Chapter 2: Internet: Online Time—Oh, and Other Media, Too." *IGen: Why Today's Super-Connected Kids Are Growing up Less Rebellious, More Tolerant, Less Happy--and Completely Unprepared for Adulthood.* Atria Books, An Imprint of Simon & Schuster, Inc., 2017.
9. Guttmann, A. "Topic: Children and Media in the U.S." *Statista*, www.statista.com/topics/3980/children-and-media-in-the-us/#topicOverview.
10. Barry, Ellen. "Social Media Use Is Linked to Brain Changes in Teens, Research Finds." *The New York Times*, 3 Jan. 2023, www.nytimes.com/2023/01/03/health/social-media-brain-adolescents.html.
11. Clement, J. "U.S. Daily Time Spent Playing Games/Computer Use by Age 2023." *Statista*, 15 Aug. 2024, www.statista.com/statistics/502149/average-daily-time-playing-games-and-using-computer-us-by-age.
12. Anderson, Monica. "Teens, Social Media and Technology 2023." *Pew Research Center*, Pew Research Center, 11 Dec. 2023, www.pewresearch.org/internet/2023/12/11/teens-social-media-and-technology-2023.
13. ConsumerAffairs. "Cell Phone Statistics 2024 [2023]" ConsumerAffairs.com. Dec. 12, 2023, https://www.consumeraffairs.com/cell_phones/cell-phone-statistics.html.
14. David L. Hill, "Why to Avoid TV for Infants and Toddlers," Healthychildren.org, American Academy of Pediatrics, October 21, 2016, www.healthychildren.org/English/family-life/Media/Pages/Why-to-Avoid-TV-Before-Age-2.aspx.
15. Hirsh-Pasek, K.Zosh, J.M., Golinkoff, R.M., Gray, J.H., Robb, M.B., & Kaufman, J. "Putting Education in "Educational" Apps: Lessons from the Science of Learning." *Psychological Science in the Public Interest.* 16(1), 3-34. 2015. https://doi.org/10.1177/1529100615569721.
16. Bowles, Nellie. "A Dark Consensus About Screens and Kids Begins to Emerge." *New York Times*, November 13, 2018. www.nytimes.com/2018/10/26/style/phones-children-silicon-valley.html.

17. Przybylski, Andrew, Amy Orben, and Netta Weinstein. "How Much Is Too Much? Examining the Relationship Between Digital Screen Engagement and Psychosocial Functioning in a Confirmatory Cohort Study," *Journal of the American Academy of Child & Adolescent Psychiatry*. June 17, 2019. https://jaacap.org/article/S0890-8567(19)31437-6/fulltext.
18. "The Dangers of Sexting." Cleveland Clinic, *Cleveland Clinic*, 25 Aug. 2024, health.clevelandclinic.org/how-to-guide-your-children-through-the-minefield-of-sexting.
19. Summer, Jay. "How Much Sleep Should a Teenager Get?" *Sleep Foundation*. 21 Dec. 2023. www.sleepfoundation.org/teens-and-sleep/how-much-sleep-does-a-teenager-need.
20. Twenge, Jean M. "Chapter 3: In Person No More: I'm with You, but Only Virtually." IGen: *Why Today's Super-Connected Kids Are Growing up Less Rebellious, More Tolerant, Less Happy--and Completely Unprepared for Adulthood*. Atria Books, An Imprint of Simon & Schuster, Inc., 2017.
21. Patchin, Justin W. "Cyberbullying Continues to Rise among Youth in the United States." *Cyberbullying Research Center*. 3 Oct. 2023. cyberbullying.org/cyberbullying-continues-to-rise-among-youth-in-the-united-states-2023.

Chapter 3

1. https://www.nytimes.com/2019/12/07/us/protect-children-online-sex-abuse.html.
2. https://www.missingkids.org/theissues/onlineenticement#bythenumbers.
3. https://www.enough.org/stats_porn_industry.
4. https://www.enough.org/stats_porn_industry.
5. https://www.enough.org/stats_porn_industry.
6. https://www.enough.org/stats_porn_industry.

Chapter 4

1. https://www.merriam-webster.com/dictionary/anxiety.
2. https://www.pewsocialtrends.org/2019/02/20/most-u-s-teens-see-anxiety-and-depression-as-a-major-problem-among-their-peers/.
3. Anderson, Monica, and Jingjing Jiang. "Teens' Social Media Habits and Experiences." *Pew Research Center.* November 28, 2018. pewresearch.org/internet/2018/11/28/teens-social-media-habits-and-experiences.
4. https://www.psychologytoday.com/us/blog/smart-people-don-t-diet/201902/teens-body-image-and-social-media.
5. Gupta, M., and Sharma, A. (2021). Fear of Missing Out: A Brief Overview of Origin, Theoretical Underpinnings and Relationship with Mental Health. *World Journal of Clinical Cases.* 9(19), 4881-4889. https://doi.org/10.12998/wjcc.v9.i19.4881.
6. https://www.momjunction.com/articles/causes-stress-teens_0010099/.
7. The NPD Group. The video game industry is adding 2-17-year-old gamers at a rate higher than that age group's population growth. Available at: http://www.afjv.com/news/233_kids-and-gaming-2011.htm.
8. Pantling, A. "Gaming Usage Up 75 percent Amid Coronavirus Outbreak, Verizon Reports." 2020. Retrieved from https://www.hollywoodreporter.com/news/gaming-usage-up-75-percent-coronavirus-outbreak-verizon-reports-1285140.
9. "Gaming Disorder: Online Q&A." World Health Organization. September 2018. www.who.int/features/qa/gaming-disorder/en.
10. https://www.psychiatry.org/patients-families/internet-gaming.
11. http://press.careerbuilder.com/2017-06-15-Number-of-Employers-Using-Social-Media-to-Screen-Candidates-at-All-Time-High-Finds-Latest-CareerBuilder-Study.

Chapter 5

1. Sedmak, A., Svetina, M. "Components of Adolescents' Attraction with YouTubers." *Curr. Psychol* 43, 6167–6179. 2024. https://doi.org/10.1007/s12144-023-04784-x.

Chapter 6

1. Brooks, Mike. "How Much Screen Time Is Too Much?" *Psychology Today*. Sussex Publishers, 1 Oct. 2023. www.psychologytoday.com/us/blog/tech-happy-life/201812/how-much-screen-time-is-too-much.
2. Shetty, Maya. "What Excessive Screen Time Does to the Adult Brain: Cognitive Enhancement." *Lifestyle Medicine*. https://longevity.stanford.edu/lifestyle/wp-content/uploads/sites/31/2023/03/Untitled-500-×-250-px-400-×-200-px-400-×-100-px-300-×-100-px.png, 5 June 2024, longevity.stanford.edu/lifestyle/2024/05/30/what-excessive-screen-time-does-to-the-adult-brain/.
3. "Charts Related to the Latest 'American Time Use Survey' News Release | More Chart Packages." *U.S. Bureau of Labor Statistics*, U.S. Bureau of Labor Statistics, www.bls.gov/charts/american-time-use/activity-by-parent.htm.

www.ingramcontent.com/pod-product-compliance
Lightning Source LLC
Chambersburg PA
CBHW061800070526
44586CB00023B/2643